Are We There Yet: Have MFAs Realized the Potential of Digital Diplomacy?

Are We There Yet: Have MFAs Realized the Potential of Digital Diplomacy?

Results from a Cross-National Comparison

By

Ilan Manor

BRILL

LEIDEN | BOSTON

Library of Congress Control Number: 2016932208

Want or need Open Access? Brill Open offers you the choice to make your research freely accessible online in exchange for a publication charge. Review your various options on brill.com/brill-open.

Typeface for the Latin, Greek, and Cyrillic scripts: "Brill". See and download: brill.com/brill-typeface.

ISBN 978-90-04-31978-3 (paperback)
ISBN 978-90-04-31979-0 (e-book)

Originally published as Volume 1(2) 2016, in *Diplomacy and Foreign Policy*, DOI 10.1163/24056006-12340002.

This book is printed on acid-free paper and produced in a sustainable manner.

Contents

Are We There Yet: Have MFAs Realized the Potential of Digital Diplomacy?

Results from a Cross-National Comparison

Ilan Manor
Department of International Development, University of Oxford

Abstract

Despite growing interest in digital diplomacy, few studies to date have evaluated the extent to which foreign ministries have been able to realize its potential. Studies have also neglected to understand the manner in which diplomats define digital diplomacy and envision its practice. This article explores the digital diplomacy model employed by four foreign ministries through interviews and questionnaires with practitioners. Results from a cross national comparison suggest that foreign ministries have been able to institutionalize the use of social media through the development of best practices and training for diplomats. However, foreign ministries seem to utilize social media to influence elite audiences rather than to foster dialogue with foreign populations. Results also suggest that both ministries and social media audiences are negotiating their respective roles in the online communication process. Although social media is used to overcome the limitations of traditional diplomacy, and manage the national image, foreign ministries fail to collaborate with non-state actors or use social media as a source of information for policy makers. Thus, while diplomacy is networked, it is still state-centric. Finally, at the embassy level, ambassadors now serve as digital gatekeepers.

Keywords

Digital Diplomacy – Public Diplomacy – Nation Branding – Social Networking Sites

* The author would like to thank Professor Juan Luis Manfredi of the University of Castilla-La Mancha, for his assistance in developing the research tools employed in this study.

 | DOI 10.1163/9789004319790_002

Introduction

On the evening of November 29, 1947, Jews throughout mandatory Palestine huddled in large groups around whatever radios could be found. Silent, they listened to a live broadcast from the UN headquarters in New York where a vote on the Partition Plan of Mandatory Palestine into two states, one Jewish and one Palestinian, was taking place. They waited in agonizing suspense as each member state voted "Yes" or "No." Their silence was shattered only a few minutes later when a majority for the Partition Plan had prevailed (Porath, 1947).

Six decades later, in July of 2015, nations at the UN headquarters in Geneva adopted a resolution regarding human rights violations in Israel's neighbor, Palestine. Rather than broadcast the individual vote of each nation, the UN social media team simply published the tweet below, which included an image of the UN scoreboard.

It is this tweet that demonstrates some of the novel features of 21st century diplomacy including the adoption of social media, the global spread of information in real time, the increased transparency of diplomatic activity and the formation of an informed online public sphere.

Recent years have seen an abundance of terms used in reference to the migration of diplomatic institutions and foreign ministries to the online world. These have included "net diplomacy," "virtual diplomacy" (Wehrenfennig, 2012), "cyber diplomacy" (Potter, 2002), "public diplomacy 2.0" (Hallams, 2010) and more recently, "digital diplomacy" (Kampf, Manor & Segev, 2015). Melissen and Hocking (2015) offer a taxonomy according to which "cyber diplomacy" deals with cyber agenda (e.g., internet freedom, cyber security) while "e-diplomacy" refers to the use of digital technologies for knowledge management and the improvement of service delivery in MFAS (e.g., consular aid). "Digital diplomacy" is a broad term that refers to the positive and negative impacts of digitalization on diplomatic institutions. As such, the term "digital diplomacy" also refers to the overall impact ICTs (information and communication technologies) have had on the practice of diplomacy, ranging from the email to the smartphone and social networking sites (or "SNS," such as Twitter and Facebook).

Recent scholarly work has begun to explore the manner in which digital diplomacy is practiced by diplomatic institutions such as embassies, foreign ministries, international organizations (e.g., the United Nations and NATO) and NGOs. While digital diplomacy has attracted scholarly work from numerous fields (international relations, communications, security studies), studies have tended to focus on its potential rather than its actual application in the field. Moreover, recent studies have failed to illustrate how diplomatic institutions have institutionalized digital technologies and what adaptations they must make to effectively use these technologies, including the need to train diplomats, develop new working routines, augment existing routines and meet the expectations of an empowered online public sphere. Finally, studies have failed to thoroughly illustrate the digital diplomacy models adopted by MFAS at both the ministry and embassy level. This study aims to address the aforementioned gaps by offering an in-depth analysis of the manner in which four MFAS have adopted, and institutionalized, the use of SNS at both the MFA and embassy level.

The theoretical perspective of this study rests on the constitutive approach to international relations as defined by Alexander Wendt (1998). This perspective was employed given the fact that diplomacy is a social institution consisting of social actors (e.g., diplomats). Thus, before digital diplomacy may be practiced, it must first be envisioned and defined by diplomats. Given its constitutive approach, this study does not seek a causal explanation to the emergence of digital diplomacy but rather explores its practice through the prism of diplomats who lend it meaning.

In line with its constitutive approach, the goal of this study is to understand how MFAs vary in their use of social media and what explains this variance. Such variance may be a result of numerous factors. For instance, highly centralized MFAs may prevent diplomats from engaging in dialogue with social media followers because they require content to be officially authorized before publication. Similarly, the manner in which MFAs view NGOs impacts the practice of digital diplomacy. Should NGOs be viewed as rivals, rather than partners, MFAs may be apprehensive in adopting networked models of diplomacy. The cost effectiveness of digital diplomacy may also result in such variance, as smaller nations may have more eagerly adopted SNS.

It is the contention of this study that realizing potential of digital diplomacy rests on an MFA's ability to a) institutionalize the use of social media by creating working routines and best practices b) reap the benefits of social media and c) overcome the challenges brought with the migration to social media. Variance in MFAs' ability to realize the potential of digital diplomacy is used to understand variance in the use of social media between MFAs.

This study proposes three research questions, each of which corresponds with its overall assertion regrading MFAs' ability to realize the potential of digital diplomacy. Thus, the first research question focused on the manner in which MFAs have institutionalized digital diplomacy through training and development of best practices. The second research question explored MFAs' ability to reap the benefits of social media and the third question examines MFAs' ability to overcome the challenges of migrating online.

In order to answer all three research questions, this study begins with a comprehensive literature review consisting of four chapters. The first identifies the events that contributed to MFAs' migration online. The second chapter illustrates the benefits of incorporating SNS into the practice of diplomacy. The third chapter identifies the challenges facing MFAs looking to migrate online while the final chapter offers a review of the existing digital diplomacy research corpus.

It should be noted that this study's literature review also offers a new prism through which one may understand digital diplomacy. In its current practice, digital diplomacy is wholly integrated into various diplomatic functions. For instance, when publishing Facebook posts on the impact trade agreements have on the US job market, the US Department of State is practicing public affairs. When launching a virtual embassy to converse with Iranians, the state department is practicing public diplomacy; and when tweeting information from deliberation rooms in Geneva, Secretary of State John Kerry is using social media in the conduct of negotiations. The incorporation of SNS in the conduct of diplomacy may therefore be blurring previously distinguishable boundaries between different forms of diplomatic practice. As such, the story of digital diplomacy may no longer be told through the prism of distinct forms of diplomacy (e.g., nation branding, public diplomacy). A more beneficial narrative explores the benefits and challenges brought about by the migration of MFAs to the online world. It is this narrative that underpins the structure of the literature review.

The study's second section introduces its research questions and methodology. In order to explore MFAs' ability to realize the potential of social media, the digital diplomacy models of four MFAs were analyzed. The study sample included the Israeli, Polish, Norwegian and Finnish MFAs. Given the constitutive approach of this study, and the understanding that digital diplomacy is practiced and imagined by social beings, the methodology employed included interviews with directors of MFA digital diplomacy units and questionnaires distributed to MFA and embassy level digital diplomacy staffers.

The third section includes an in-depth description of the four digital diplomacy models adopted by the MFAs that participated in this study. While the term "digital diplomacy" refers to numerous technologies and ICTs, this study focuses solely on the incorporation of social media and SNS into the practice of diplomacy. Social media (e.g., blogs, Wikis) may be defined as a set of online tools that are centered on social interaction and facilitate two-way communication (Lee & Kwak, 2012) while SNS (e.g., Twitter, Facebook) are defined as "web based services that allow individuals to (1) construct a public or semi-public profile within a bounded system, (2) articulate a list of other users with whom they share a connection, and (3) view and traverse their list of connections and those made by others within the system" (Boyd & Ellison, 2007).

Given that this study focuses solely on social media and SNS, it adopts the broad definition offered by Bjola and Holmes (2015). According to their definition, digital diplomacy consists of three components: ways in which actors engage with audiences to project an image or message (the public diplomacy and nation branding component), ways in which MFAs structure and organize information for diplomats and constituents (the institutionalization of social media) and ways in which actors monitor changes in political structures and public opinion (the information gathering component). Each of these components was used in order to analyze, de-construct and illustrate MFA digital diplomacy models at both the ministry and embassy levels. These four models, in turn, help solve the puzzle of variance in the use and adoption of social media by MFAs.

The fourth and final section offers a comprehensive discussion with regard to this study's findings, their contribution to the study of digital diplomacy and areas in which additional research is necessary.

Literature Review

The Need for Digital Diplomacy

Reviewing the existing literature enables one to identify four events that resonate across the research corpus as contributing to the advent of digital diplomacy.

Countering al-Qaeda's grand narrative. One of the main drivers of digital diplomacy was al-Qaeda's use of the internet and social media to spread its grand narrative, which stated that Osama bin Laden and his followers were agents of Islamic history who would reverse the decline of the Muslim world and defeat Western imperialism (Hallams, 2010). Through websites, blogs and video sermons disseminated online, al-Qaeda promoted its narrative among a community that flourished online while its bases were bombarded offline. Al-Qaeda was thus also able to brand itself as an omnipotent terror organization withstanding the might of the world's strongest nations (ibid.). The importance of countering this narrative became evident in a 2008 estimate stating that the internet is responsible for 80% of the recruitment of youth for jihadi groups (Hallams, 2010, p. 544). Realizing the need to migrate online, Karen Hughes, President George W. Bush's Undersecretary of State for Public Diplomacy and Public Affairs, launched Public Diplomacy 2.0, an initiative which sought to win the war of ideas through digital diplomacy. To this end, the state department launched a Facebook page, opened an official blog and created a Digital Outreach Team tasked with countering al-Qaeda's narrative on Arab language websites and forums (ibid., 2010).

The Arab Spring. The democratic revolts that swept through the Middle East during 2011 further motivated governments to adopt social media (Stein, 2011; Seib, 2012; Causey & Howard, 2013). As Seib argues, world governments were taken by surprise by the Arab Spring as foreign policy decision makers were not monitoring the information ecology in which these revolts were taking shape—that of social media. While SNS did not cause these uprisings, they did enable citizens to air their frustration with totalitarian regimes amid like-minded audiences (Seib, 2012) and mobilize protestors on the ground (Stein, 2011; Sotiriu, 2015). Not only did governments fail to monitor SNS, but most relied on state-owned media channels which depicted a divergent reality to that which was unfolding in Tahrir Square (Seib, 2012). In the wake of 2011, governments realized that social media can serve as an intelligence tool for diplomats looking to understand and anticipate events (ibid., 2012; Causey & Howard, 2013).

The rise of citizen journalists. The global proliferation of ICTs such as smartphones with cameras has enabled every individual to become a one-person news supplier able to disseminate information to a global audience (Seib, 2012). Causey and Howard state that citizen journalists may provide real-time, on-the-ground information from conflict zones, a realization that prompted the Voice of America, the U.S. federal government's broadcast institution, to integrate user-generated content into its coverage of Iran's 2009 Green Revolution (Xiguang & Jing, 2010). Similarly, during the Arab Spring, news network Al Jazeera supplemented its coverage with user-generated content (Seib, 2012). During these protests, citizen journalists offered a narrative of the Arab uprisings that contradicted that of the state, thereby impacting the framing of events (Meraz & Papacharissi, 2013). The ability of citizen journalists to provide real-time information from conflict zones, coupled with their influence over the coverage of world events, further motivated MFAs to migrate to SNS.

A new media ecology. Hayden maintains that the new technological landscape, brought about by ICTs and social media technologies, was also a driver of digital diplomacy. According to Hayden, MFAs are in need of a "new" public diplomacy that contends with a global media ecology characterized by the fragmentation of audiences to networks of selective exposure (Hayden, 2012; Williamson & Kelley, 2012). Overcoming the fragmentation of diplomacy's audiences may be achieved by incorporating social media into the practice of public diplomacy. However, Hayden states that the characteristics of social media will inevitably impact the culture of diplomacy. Social media are virtual platforms where issues may be debated and defined (Park & Reber, 2008; Smith, 2010). The dialogic and interactive characteristics of social media necessitate a shift in the culture of diplomacy as the goal of public diplomacy is transformed from transmission of information to building and leveraging of relationships with foreign publics (Hayden, 2012). The centrality of relationships in Hayden's "new" public diplomacy is emblematic of a larger paradigmatic shift in the conceptualization of public diplomacy that shall be expanded on in the next section.

The Benefits of Digital Diplomacy

A new public diplomacy? Traditionally, public diplomacy was conceptualized as influence over foreign public opinion that would impact the conduct of diplomacy. Early definitions of the term state that nations should influence the opinions of elite groups in foreign nations, which would then impact their governments' policies (Pamment, 2013). The 9/11 terror attacks led to a global debate on the virtues of public diplomacy given the fact that the Bush administration's war on terror was also a war over the "heart and minds" of the Muslim world (Melissen, 2005). Post-9/11 definitions of "public diplomacy" capture a conceptual shift among public diplomacy scholars and practitioners which places an emphasis on engaging with foreign populations. Cull (2008) asserts that the term "public diplomacy" refers to the process by which international actors seek to accomplish their foreign policy goals by engaging with foreign publics. Melissen defines the new public diplomacy as one that focuses on engaging with increasingly "connected" publics while transitioning from one-way flows of information towards dialogue, engagement and long-term relationship building (Melissen, 2005; Pamment, 2013).

Pamment argues that while 20th century public diplomacy was characterized by one-way flows of information and limited interaction between communicator and recipient, two-way communication is the very essence of the "new" public diplomacy, which is dialogic, inclusive and collaborative (Pamment, 2013, p. 3). The "new" public diplomacy thus represents a clear break from the one-way broadcasting model of public diplomacy (ibid., 2013) and transitions from monologue to dialogue (Cowan & Arsenault, 2008). Seo (2013) writes that the relational approach to public diplomacy (i.e., one that places emphasis on fostering relations with foreign populations) differs from past approaches as it engages citizens rather than elites.

Gregory amply summarizes this conceptual transition by stating that public diplomacy is now an instrument used by states, associations of states and non-state actors to understand cultures, attitudes and behaviors, to build and manage relationships and to mobilize actions that advance one's interests (Gregory, 2011, p. 353). The relational approach to public diplomacy stems from communication theories that place an emphasis on the communicative act itself. In this regard, the goal of dialogue with online publics may be dialogue itself rather than persuasion (Brown, 2013; Causey & Howard, 2013).

The potential of two-way public diplomacy also stems from its ethical dimension (Zhang, 2013). Grunig's "Excellence Theory" states that two-way symmetrical communication is ethical, as it requires mutual understanding between organizations and publics, thus allowing public attitudes to influence the behaviors of organizations (Grunig & Hunt, 1984; Comor & Bean, 2012; Zhang, 2013). Ociepka (2012) and Brown (2013) argue that traditional public diplomacy activities were related to propaganda and information dominance and were thus viewed as unethical. However, the use of symmetrical communication between MFAs and foreign populations is both legitimate and ethical, given a commitment to mutuality, trust building, symmetry and dialogue.

Social media and SNS may be the very tools for the practice of the "new" public diplomacy as they enable organizations to transition from "broadcast" to "communicative" paradigms that are centered on interaction with online users (McNutt, 2014). SNS such as Twitter and Facebook are particularly relevant to the "new" public diplomacy as relationships are the foundations of social networking sites (Waters et al., 2009). Moreover, SNS provide ideal conditions for two-way engagement as organizations may communicate with individuals on topics of shared interest (Bortree & Seltzer, 2009).

In recent years, MFAs and embassies throughout the world have flocked to SNS such as Twitter and Facebook. According to the Twiplomacy website, there are more than 200 MFAs and foreign ministers active on Twitter in addition to some 400 heads of state and more than 200 missions to UN institutions (Twiplomacy, 2015). While the digital diplomacy research corpus tends to be America-centric, the adoption of social media by MFAs is a global phenomenon. Arab MFAs such as Egypt, Qatar, Jordan and Bahrain all operate official Twitter accounts. Similarly, countries such as Nigeria, Kenya, Ethiopia, South Africa and Botswana are all active on SNS (Manor, 2015). Even the digital divide seems to be narrowing in digital diplomacy as some African countries (e.g., Ethiopia, Kenya, Somalia) are just as active as their Western peers on social media (Kampf, Manor & Segev, 2015). For some MFAs, the very use of web 2.0 applications is a goal in itself, as it projects a certain national image. Natarajan (2014) states, that by its mere presence on social media, India is crafting an image of a global and connected "new India" (Natarajan, 2014).

Yet migrating to social media does not guarantee that one practices digital diplomacy. Such a practice rests on an MFA's willingness to interact with online publics through engagement and listening.

Between engagement, listening and tailoring. The drivers of digital diplomacy (e.g., Arab Spring, al-Qaeda's narrative) crystallized MFAs' need to interact with SNS users assembled in the new online public sphere. As Judith McHale, President Barack Obama's Under Secretary of State for Public Diplomacy and Public Affairs, stated:

> *In a world where power and influence truly belongs to the many, we must engage with more people in more places... people all around the world are clamoring to be heard... they are having important conversations rights now... and they aren't waiting for us.* (Hayden, 2012)

McHale's statement identifies the most important components of digital diplomacy: engagement and listening (Kampf, Manor & Segev, 2015). According to

Metzgar (2012), "engagement" refers to the need to communicate with online publics assembled in various networks while "listening" refers to the use of SNS to understand foreign populations and shape foreign policy accordingly. Listening to online publics also enables MFAs to gauge public opinion and anticipate events (Ociepka, 2012).

Metzgar's argument highlights another benefit of digital diplomacy, namely the ability to tailor foreign policy messages to the unique characteristics of target audiences such as language, culture and values (Metzgar, 2012; Seo, 2013). Such tailoring may increase the target audience's willingness to interact with an MFA or embassy. Effective tailoring rests on one's ability to identify specific target audiences, communication channels and platforms (Xiguang & Jing, 2010). Ociepka (2012) asserts that through tailoring, social media have changed the practice of public diplomacy as both mass and niche audiences are targeted. Finally, nations may also tailor SNS content based on the manner in which they are perceived by foreign audiences. By listening to local SNS users, nations may understand how they are viewed by local populations and shape social media content in an attempt to manage their image. Thus, social media is one way to promote a positive national image and a tailored persona (Harris, 2013). In the age of SNS, such personas may be referred to as "selfies."

On selfie diplomacy. Nation branding may be defined as a "process by which a nation's image can be created, monitored, evaluated and proactively managed in order to improve or enhance the country's reputation among a target international audience" (Fan, 2012). Image is what people recognize as most central about their nation while reputation is a form of feedback received from the outside world regarding a nation's identity claims (ibid., 2010). Manor & Segev (2015) argue that nation branding is a nation's attempt to draw its self-portrait. As self-portraits depicted on SNS are known as selfies, they refer to nation branding via SNS as "selfie diplomacy."

Selfie diplomacy is now common practice as MFAs and embassies market their nations in connected, yet increasingly competitive, environments (Stein, 2011). India's MFA, for instance, uses social media to promote documentary films showcasing India's history and culture (Natarajan, 2014). Similarly, the #WAVE campaign (World against Violence and Extremism) currently promoted on the Twitter account of Iranian President Hassan Rouhani aims to present Iran as a stabilizing force in the region.

Another possible example of selfie diplomacy is the Hamas movement's Twitter Q&A session held during March of 2015 (Deitch, 2015). Hamas is a diplomatic anomaly given that Israel, the US, Japan and Australia all designate it a terror organization while other countries consider its political wing to be the elected representative of Palestinians living in Gaza. Thus, it is unclear if Hamas's Q&A session was an example of public diplomacy, in which governments engage with foreign populations, or a form of selfie diplomacy, in which a terror organization seeks to re-brand itself. By using Twitter, the Hamas brand may have acquired traits associated with Twitter's brand, such as freedom of speech and democracy. Through dialogue with SNS followers, Hamas may have also altered its image from a terror organization to a liberation movement, as terrorists are known for violence and not public scrutiny or dialogue with those who oppose them. Finally, many of the questions raised by followers were answered by a female Hamas representative, thereby enabling it to distinguish itself from other Islamic groups—such as Daesh—which are associated with the oppression of women (Manor, 2015).

The use of Q&A sessions in selfie diplomacy demonstrates that many digital diplomacy activities rest on dialogue. However, as noted in the next section, such dialogue is often limited by diplomatic institutions.

Practicing dialogue. The acceptance of engagement and listening as fundamental components of digital diplomacy means that one cannot measure the effectiveness of digital diplomacy by the number of "Likes" on an MFA's Facebook profile. Rather, one must evaluate the scope of dialogue between the MFA and its SNS followers (Metzgar, 2012; Kampf, Manor & Segev, 2015).

Like the Hamas movement, the majority of diplomatic institutions practice dialogue in the form of SNS Q&A sessions. Recent examples of such sessions include a Twitter panel with five Arctic Ambassadors (Norway, Iceland, Finland, Sweden and Denmark) organized by Twitter, a Twitter Q&A session with the president of the UN's Human Rights Council, and a Twitter Q&A session between the US state department and US citizens seeking to travel to Cuba following the re-establishment of diplomatic ties.

Kampf, Manor and Segev (2015) have argued that Q&A sessions are a form of quarantined engagement, as they deal with a single issue. An example of open MFA-to-public engagement took place on the 12th of February, 2015, as the US state department held a Q&A session with its spokesperson Jen Psaki. This session was open and not limited in scope. SNS users asked questions regarding a wide array of issues, such as climate change, US-Taliban relations and US aid to civilians in South Sudan. Online Q&A sessions demonstrate the potential of digital diplomacy to foster two-way dialogic communication between diplomatic institutions and online publics. Online engagement may also add to the credibility of diplomatic institutions, as it demonstrates a willingness to increase transparency (Wichowski, 2015) and confront criticism.

In May 2014, the European Union's embassy to Israel held a Facebook Q&A session with its ambassador. Questions dealt with the EU's lax response to the Crimean crisis, its unwillingness to intervene in the Syrian civil war and its intention to recognize the Hamas movement as a legitimate government. This conversation highlights another benefit of digital diplomacy—the ability to circumvent the local press (Natarajan, 2014). By engaging directly with Israelis, the ambassador was able to narrate, or frame, the EU's policies without going through the national media, which adds its own interpretation to issues. Diplomats' ability to frame government action through SNS is explored in the next section.

Framing the nation. The Pew Research Center's 2015 journalism and media survey found that the majority of Americans use Twitter and Facebook as their main source of information on events outside personal life (Pew, 2015). The growing use of social media as a news source demonstrates government's ability to offer SNS followers its own interpretation of events, which may be at odds with that presented by news outlets. Such interpretations may be regarded as frames. To frame, according to Entman, is "to select some aspects of a perceived reality and make them more salient in a communicating text, in such a way as to promote a particular problem definition, causal interpretation, moral evaluation and/or treatment recommendation for the item described" (Entman, 1993).

In order to demonstrate how governments frame issues, Entman (2003) proposes the Cascading Activation Model, in which a frame extends from the White House to the public while passing through elites and the press (See Appendix 1). The model illustrates two factors. The first is the government's dependency on elites and news outlets who may or may not push a frame down the cascade to the public. The second is a feedback cycle in which the media offers insight regarding the public's acceptance of government frames.

But this model may no longer explain the relationship between government, media and the public. SNS users following MFAs are directly exposed to governmental framing and no longer rely on the media to interpret events. Likewise, governments receive direct feedback from their SNS followers in the forms of Facebook "Likes" or comments. It should be stated that SNS users may choose to follow governments, the media and citizen journalists who have risen to the role of information gatekeepers (Meraz & Papacharissi, 2013). Thus, social media is best understood as a contested arena in which each actor promotes his framing of events (Hamdy & Gomaa, 2012).

Van Ham (2013) argues that framing is a key instrument in the "new" public diplomacy, as this is the diplomacy of norms and values. Van Ham's understanding of public diplomacy rests on the concept of social power, which he defines as the ability to set standards and create norms and values that are deemed as legitimate and desirable, without resorting to coercion or payment. Wielding social power is the use of frames in order to construct new norms or values to which other nations must adhere, thereby limiting the actions of other nations. Thus, framing is a competitive process in which wielders of social power attempt to convince audiences that their interpretation of events is the correct one. Natarajan (2014) argues that the establishment of norms limits the state's branding ability, as it cannot project a narrative that contradicts accepted values and norms.

Using social media to bypass traditional news outlets and communicate directly with domestic and foreign audiences is but one manner in which digital diplomacy enables MFAs to overcome the limitations of traditional diplomacy.

Overcoming limitations of traditional diplomacy. An important benefit of digital diplomacy is the use of SNS to complement traditional foreign policy tools (Seo, 2013). As part of the 21st Century Statecraft initiative, the US state department sought to overcome the limitations of traditional diplomacy vis-à-vis its relations with Iran. Given that both nations had no diplomatic ties for 30 years, the US was unable to engage with Iranian citizens, narrate its foreign policy and shape its image. In December of 2011 the department launched Virtual Embassy Tehran, a web-based platform that served as a virtual embassy enabling the US to converse online with Iranians and offer information regarding US values and history (Metzgar, 2012). Similarly, in 2013 Israel launched its own virtual embassy on Twitter, hoping to engage with the populations of six Gulf nations with whom Israel has no diplomatic relations (Ravid, 2013).

Additionally, digital diplomacy enables MFAs and nations to reconnect with their diaspora, thus overcoming spatial limitations of diplomacy. Diaspora diplomacy aims to engage a country's overseas community in order to build relationships with foreign countries (Rana, 2013). Diaspora's role in diplomacy has risen to prominence given the steady growth of migrant communities (Attias, 2012). China, India, Mexico and Israel are examples of nations that now practice diaspora diplomacy in terms of meeting the needs of expats, mobilizing them to achieve foreign policy goals, encouraging them to trade with their country of origin and using diasporas as a source of intelligence gathering (Attias, 2012; Zaharna, Arsenault & Fisher, 2013; Clarke, 2015). Migrants who have connections within their host country, as well as with their country of origin, are members of transitional networks that may be leveraged by states. As such, diaspora diplomacy is but one example of networked diplomacy, a concept elaborated on in the following section.

Networked and collaborative approaches to diplomacy. The concept of networked diplomacy is anchored in two main arguments. The first is that the globalized world is a complex one in which challenges transcend borders (e.g., food security, climate change) and no nation can address such challenges alone (Copeland, 2013). The second argument states that networks have become the organizing structure of societies (Castells, 2011). As networks are characterized by lack of hierarchy, the nation state is losing power to other nodes in the network, such as connected individuals and NGOs. Copeland (2013) states that power is migrating upwards, outwards and downwards.

Zaharna, Arsenault and Fisher (2013) state that a 21st century approach to diplomacy must recognize the architecture of multi-hub, multi-directional networks that exist around the world, transcend borders and are maintained by social media. This web of networks offers valuable connections between governments, corporations, organizations and individuals who contribute to the global agenda (Slaughter, 2009). Such was the case with the British foreign office's global campaign to end sexual violence in conflict (Pamment, 2015).

Networking also fosters innovation (Slaughter, 2009; Park & Lim, 2014). MFAs may form global networks in which ideas and innovations are nurtured in order to overcome global challenges (Lalani, 2011). Zaharna, Arsenault and Fisher (2013) view networked diplomacy as collaborative in nature.

Networks are not a new concept in diplomacy. Indeed, the Catholic Church has long operated as a global network in which information was passed through an interconnected web of papal legates and cardinals (The Economist, 2015). What is new is the multi-stakeholder environment in which network diplomacy is now practiced, as it includes the newsroom elite, civil society, NGOs and individuals. Collaborating and fostering relationships with these stakeholders may be achieved through two-way interaction and dialogue made possible by SNS (Hayden, 2012).

Collaborative approaches to public diplomacy may be a necessity given the newfound agency of SNS users. As Zaharna and Rugh (2012) assert, SNS users are more likely to be producers of content than consumers since participation has replaced passivity as the main characteristic of public diplomacy audiences. Williamson and Kelly (2012) state that the collaborative nature of social media has increased an individual's sense of agency given his ability to exchange ideas and co-create content. For MFAs, this sense of agency may be a double-edged sword. While collaborative environments enhance SNS users' desire to engage with diplomats, failure to collaborate with followers may reduce their sense of agency, leading them to abandon MFA social media profiles (Kampf, Manor & Segev, 2015).

Finally, collaborative diplomacy may pave the way to peer-to-peer (P2P) diplomacy in which citizens create or disseminate MFA social media content among their own social networks (Attias, 2012). P2P diplomacy is seen as especially beneficial, given that people may be more receptive to messages authored by their online "friends" than those authored by governmental institutions, which could be viewed as "Twipoganda" (Saunders, 2013; Zaharna, Arsenault & Fisher, 2013; Kampf, Manor & Segev, 2015). Collaborations between MFAs and their online followers may also increase ministries' ability to provide consular aid in times of emergency.

Consular aid. The digital diplomacy research corpus has tended to overlook the issue of SNS-based consular assistance. Yet consular aid demonstrates tan MFA's relevance to the domestic population. Likewise, the use of SNS in crisis management is effective, as organizations and individuals can exchange relevant information in real time (Harris, 2013).

Kenya's foreign ministry seems to be especially attuned to the consular needs of its citizens. On the 18th of December 2013, as internal fighting broke out in South Sudan, Kenya's MFA published a tweet stating that citizens in need of assistance evacuating from the country could contact the Kenyan ambassador. The tweet included the ambassador's phone number. On the 19th of December, the Kenyan MFA used Twitter yet again in order to disseminate information on flights leaving South Sudan while also answering questions posted by Kenyan nationals (Kampf, Manor & Segev, 2015; Manor, 2015). As Harris concludes, social media enables real-time response to events, therefore adding strategic value to the use of social media in diplomacy (Harris, 2013).

Natarajan (2014) states that public diplomacy works in two different time frames. Short term public diplomacy focuses on events taking place in real time (e.g., evacuation of citizens during civil unrest) while long term public diplomacy is used to create a coherent national narrative. MFAs' response to the 2015 Nepal earthquake demonstrates both these time frames with relation to digital diplomacy.

Within hours of the earthquake, the UK Foreign & Commonwealth Office launched a webpage detailing the manner in which British nationals in Nepal could contact the foreign office by email, phone or an online form. In addition, the foreign office tweeted "#Nepal earthquake: British Nationals requiring consular assistance please call +44 (0) 207 008 0000 or text NEPAL to +447860010026". Soon, British nationals were using Twitter to communicate directly with the foreign office. Similarly, the US state department also took to Twitter in order to publish the details of a special email address to which all requests for assistance from US nationals should be sent. Interestingly, the state department used the hashtags #NepalQauke and #NepaklEarthquake which were already trending on Twitter, thereby enabling it to reach a larger number of citizens (Harris, 2013). Alternatively, Canada's MFA chose to employ crowdsourcing, asking its citizens to re-tweet MFA social media content.

In addition to offering consular aid, MFAs began organizing aid missions to Nepal. In the days following the earthquake, the Canadian and Israeli MFAs regularly tweeted images of their aid missions. As the short term goal of aiding citizens had been largely achieved, MFAs turned to their long time goal of image management.

Crisis management through social media demonstrates Hocking and Melissen's (2015) assertion that online and offline diplomacy are not mutually exclusive but complementary. Citizens in need of aid offline may reach out to MFAs online, and agencies delivering aid offline may locate people in need online (Abbasi, Kumar, Andrade Filho & Liu, 2012). The integration of offline and online diplomacy may be referred to as "hybrid diplomacy" (Hocking & Melissen, 2015). Hocking and Melissen further argue that in diplomacy, new forms of communication do not utterly supplant older, more tested means of communication. Rather, they are used to increase diplomatic efficacy.

The benefits of digital diplomacy expanded on in this section are summarized in the image below.

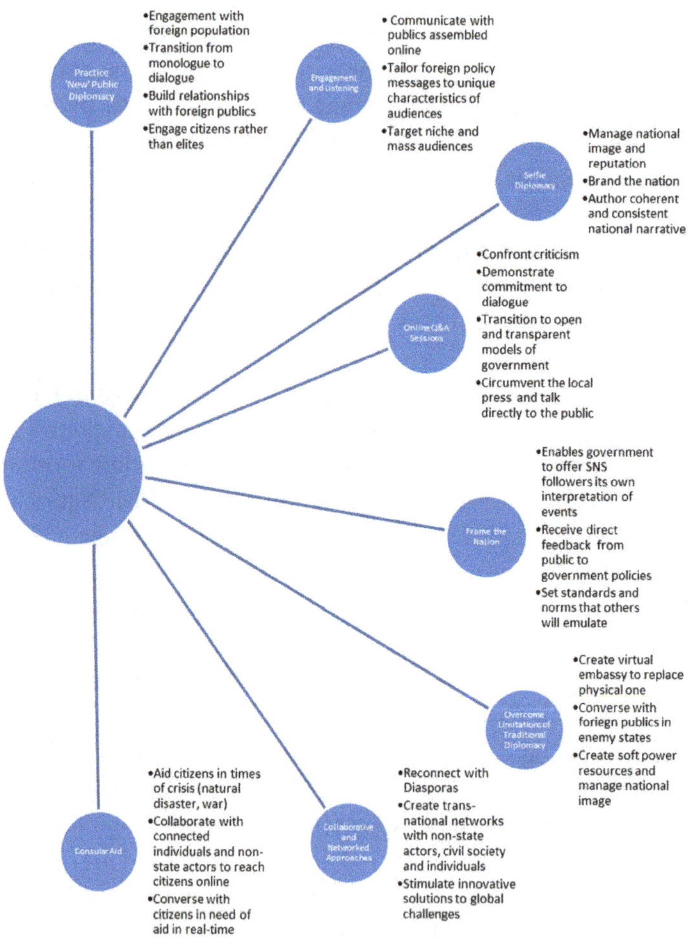

The benefits of digital diplomacy

Social media technologies enable governments to form coalitions with stakeholders, provide assistance to citizens, create ties with diasporas, manage their images and foster relationships with foreign populations. Yet practicing digital diplomacy also calls on MFAs to overcome great challenges. These challenges are presented in the next section.

The Challenges of Digital Diplomacy

Migrating online. Recent scholarly work has tended to regard diplomacy as an island onto itself focusing solely on MFAs' migration online. Yet digital diplomacy scholarship may benefit from a wider viewpoint, according to which MFAs are but one branch of government trying to establish an online presence. Thus, the challenges MFAs face are relevant to all governmental ministries that have migrated online in programs collectively referred to as "E-gov initiatives" (Belanger & Carter, 2005).

The migration of government to cyberspace brought with it novel challenges, such as guarding citizens' private information (Scott, 2012) and securing critical infrastructure against cyber threats (Quigley, 2013). Similarly, web 2.0 applications (e.g., websites, blogs, SNS) have also brought with them challenges, as governments cannot simply replicate existing working routines from the offline world to online participatory environments (McNutt, 2014). McNutt uses the term "government 2.0" in reference to a technological functionality as well as the embrace of a web 2.0 ethos composed of transparency, participatory opportunities, co-production and openness. As part of this ethos, governments must engage with citizens while valuing their comments and ideas (Macnamara, Sakinofsky & Beattie, 2011; Macnamara, 2012).

McNutt's web 2.0 ethos demonstrates that MFAs are not the only branch of government making the transition from monologic to dialogic modes of communication. McNutt identifies three barriers to the adoption of a web 2.0 ethos by government ministries. First, resources may prove a barrier, as ministries must seek out engagement with citizens while providing updated information. Secondly, the use of social media necessitates the formation of best practices for employees now operating in unfamiliar environments. The third barrier is normative, as government culture is risk averse. Thus, governments may be reluctant to embrace SNS given fear of losing control over the communication process. While the barriers identified by McNutt are relevant to all government institutions, the following section evaluates their relevance to MFAs.

The need for resources. Following the end of the Cold War, MFAs found themselves operating in a changed environment characterized by growing demands alongside shrinking resources. The search for cost effective diplomacy led to interest in "virtual" diplomacy (Hocking & Melissen, 2015). In recent years, many have argued that digital diplomacy, delivered through social media, is indeed cost effective (Causey & Howard, 2013; Copeland, 2013; Pamment, 2015). However, when evaluating the current practice of digital diplomacy, its cost effectiveness may be questioned.

In 2012, it was estimated that the US state department managed some 288 Facebook profiles, 200 Twitter accounts and 125 YouTube channels. Fergus Hanson argued that these amounted to a social media empire (Hayden, 2012). According to the 2014 annual report by the US Advisory Commission on Public Diplomacy, the state department's social media empire has grown by 50% and now includes 1,000 accounts. As the goal of the "new" public diplomacy is to actively engage in dialogue with online audiences, the department must use each of these channels to answer followers' questions, respond to criticism and provide information. Yet producing appealing SNS content requires time, effort and a dedicated staff (Archetti, 2012).

The US state department is not the only MFA to manage a social media empire. MFAs such as Sweden, Germany, Japan and Kenya are all active on numerous platforms, as is the UK foreign office, which operates a global blogosphere. The costs associated with digital diplomacy continue to rise if one takes into account the activities of the other governmental agencies and institutions that also commonly have an effect on a nation's image and may impact relationships between nations. In the United States' case, these include the Central Intelligence Agency, the Centers for Disease Control and Prevention, the House Committee on Foreign Affairs and NASA, which alone operates 500 SNS channels (Stockton, 2015).

The online activity of numerous governmental ministries, agencies and national leaders poses another challenge to MFAs, which may be referred to as "plurality of channels." As each of these actors publishes content that deals with a nation's foreign policy, and which may influence the national image, MFAs find themselves operating in contested environments in which they are no longer the sole author of the national narrative. For instance, the European Union's digital diplomacy apparatus includes the Twitter accounts of the European Commission, the European parliament, the president of the European Council, the high representative of the Union for Foreign Affairs and Security Policy, and numerous European agencies (e.g., EU Climate Action), not to mention the EU's embassies and ambassadors around the world. Plurality of channels suggests that the digital age has rendered MFAs an incoherent narrator, to paraphrase Shenhav, Sheafer and Gabay (2010). Overcoming this challenge requires MFAs to coordinate their public diplomacy and nation branding activities with the multitude of national actors now operating online. In 2006, Israel attempted to do just that by establishing a "national public diplomacy forum" meant to coordinate all content disseminated by national ministries (Molad, 2012).

An additional challenge brought on by MFAs' migration online is the need to develop digital skill sets among diplomats, many of whom are more accustomed to an analog world. This challenge is explored in the next section.

Best practices and training. Practicing digital diplomacy necessitates the formulation of guidelines and best practices that may aid diplomats venturing onto social media (Vance, 2012; McNutt, 2014). In recent years, organizations such as the US Marine Corps, US Department of Defense, UK Foreign & Commonwealth Office and the governments of Canada and New Zealand have all formulated such guidelines.

Digital diplomacy also requires training and the acquisition of new skills (Vance, 2012). Training of senior diplomats may be of special significance, as they are at the forefront of digital diplomacy. For instance, Twitter Q&A sessions regularly feature ambassadors, as they are their country's official representative abroad authorized to speak on behalf of their nation. Yet training ambassadors may prove a substantial drain on resources given their lack of familiarity with digital environments. As seniority comes with age, many high-ranking diplomats are "digital immigrants," or people who grew up in an analog world who are now attempting to adapt to a digital one (Presnky, 2011). Thus, they lack the intuitive ability of "digital natives" to master the operation of social media technologies. Training, however, is also relevant to digital natives. While these may easily master the use of social media, they must learn when, where and how one can use these tools in order to manage change in the international environment (Williamson & Kelly, 2012).

Lastly, both digital natives and immigrants need to be trained in digital diplomacy literacy. Digital literacy has been defined as the variety of technical, cognitive and sociological skills necessary in order to perform tasks and solve problems in digital environments (Eshet-Alkalai, 2004, p. 93). Similarly, this study defines "digital diplomacy literacy" as the ability to extract all information that is hidden in a 140 character tweet. The following tweet, published by the German MFA on the 12th of March 2014, illustrates digital diplomacy literacy.

This was the first tweet by any MFA to include the hashtag "G7," announcing the expulsion of Russia from the G8 group given its incursion into Crimea. The G7 hashtag also demonstrated that these seven nations decided to act in unison and would all reject the results of a Crimean referendum. By using the words "#Crimea+other parts," this tweet confirmed reports that Russian forces had entered other parts of Ukraine. Finally, while this tweet identified Russia as responsible for the crisis, it also outlined a diplomatic solution—Russia

could de-escalate the crisis by retreating from Ukrainian territory. Thus, this one tweet summarizes an entire foreign policy agenda.

While MFAs may use social media to articulate new foreign policies, these may be received both positively and negatively by online publics. Such a possible loss over the communication process clashes with MFAs' overall risk averse culture, which is explored in the next section.

MFA's risk averse culture. Copeland (2013) characterizes MFAs as change-resistant institutions that are disconnected, inadequately resourced and without a domestic constituency given that they face outwards with their back to the capital. Copeland's characterization of MFAs explains why the transition from monologic to dialogic public diplomacy is not a natural one. Yet technology has always impacted the practice of diplomacy and the organizational cultures of MFAs. Throughout the 20th century, the emergence of mass media technologies such as the radio led to a deep rooted organizational culture in which MFAs focused on one-way communication models with the aim of informing and influencing foreign audiences (Zaharna, Arsenault & Fisher, 2013). The characteristics of mass media are incompatible with relationship-building, as they target the largest possible audience, feedback is delayed and audiences are assumed to be passive (ibid., 2013).

Unlike 20th century diplomacy, digital diplomacy calls on MFAs to forge relationships with online publics that are well informed, opinionated, clamoring to be heard and volatile. The unpredictability of online audiences and the fear of losing control over the communication process may inhibit MFAs' ability to realize the potential of SNS (Zaharna & Rugh, 2012; Ogawa, 2013).

Such loss of control was evident in May of 2014, as Michelle Obama tweeted a selfie holding the sign "#BringBackOurGirls" referencing the abduction of 250 Nigerian school girls by the Islamic Boko Haram group.

While Obama's selfie garnered more than 56 thousand re-tweets, it was met with criticism from SNS followers who mounted a counter social media campaign in which they shared their selfies with the sign "#BringBackYourDrones," referencing the Obama administration's frequent use of drones in its war on terror. These followers effectively rejected Obama's message, arguing that the US's use of drones was as immoral as Boko Haram's actions. Moreover, rather than focus attention on the fate of the girls, Obama's selfie reignited the debate surrounding the morality of the US's war on terror (Manor, 2014). This

is emblematic of Haynal's (2011) assertion that a technologically empowered audience is asserting itself in unpredictable yet powerful ways.

However, this example also illustrates potential benefits of digital diplomacy. First, hashtag activism may influence the media's agenda (Scott, 2015). Obama's tweet may have therefore brought media attention to the fate of the abducted girls. Secondly, US first ladies are senior political figures. Thus, Obama's tweet, which was disseminated by the state department and made its way via Twitter to foreign embassies in DC, constitutes an official statement by the US that freeing the Nigerian girls is a foreign policy priority. Finally, the #BringBackYourDrones campaign highlighted the fact that America's reliance on drones was viewed by foreign populations as a moral blemish and was perhaps hindering the US's goal of promoting dialogue with the Muslim world. Herein lies the value of listening to online publics. As Nicholas Cull writes, "*the actor would do well to identify the points where foreign opinion and its own foreign policy part company, and work hard to close the gap or explain the divergence*" (Cull, 2008, p. 47).

While McNutt (2014) argues that government culture is risk averse, Wichowski (2015) characterizes MFA culture as secretive, putting it at odds with societal norms and causing a culture clash.

A Culture clash. Wichowski (2015) argues that in a quest to be safe, government is becoming more secretive and that secrecy is a culture in which one operates. Yet the digital age has created a culture of sharing in which people share both impersonal and personal information. The sharing society is in stark contradiction to MFAs' secretive culture. This contradiction has intensified as people now expect governments to share information with them (ibid., 2015). Information sharing is also the basis of relational approaches to public diplomacy, as it enables symmetrical communication with an informed partner (Kent & Taylor, 1998). MFAs' secretive culture may therefore inhibit their ability to realize the potential of digital diplomacy (Wichowski, 2015).

The secretive culture of diplomacy is not the only element influencing MFAs' information sharing practices. As Bjola (2014) explains, secrecy is often a pre-requisite for diplomacy, even in the digital age. Secret diplomacy may unlock peace negotiations by insulating leaders and creating an environment that is more conducive for dialogue; preventing dangerous escalations between nations; and providing incentives for normalizing adversarial relations. However, at a time when even the CIA is tweeting its way to the limelight, the pressure on governments to be more transparent is mounting. Pressure is also mounting on governments to react to real time events in near real time.

The need for time versus real-time diplomacy. Seib (2012) argues that the Arab Spring highlighted a temporal interference in the conduct of diplomacy, as social media and ICTs increase the speed with which revolutions and world events take place. The all-powerful Hosni Mubarak was ousted in three weeks while the Ukrainian Orange Revolution lasted only two weeks. Likewise, in the global media ecology, one video from a demonstration in Damascus can circle the globe within a matter of hours. As such, connected publics expect governments to immediately comment on world events as they unfold while policy makers find themselves operating in a non-stop news cycle. Seib refers to this temporal interference as "real-time diplomacy."

The need for real-time diplomacy is at odds with diplomacy's need for time. Reaching foreign policy decisions that influence national interests requires that information be verified with other governmental bodies and insights be pooled from various departments and agencies. This brings about delays in commenting or acting in response to world events, especially when compared to media outlets and NGOs (Soltzfus, 2008). The time lag between NGOs and MFAs may also stem from the fact that NGOs may have better access to information, as they have volunteers "on the ground." This access to information, as well as the ability to act without conferring with other bodies, allows NGOs and the media to react to events in near real time and frame events in a manner consistent with their agenda (Soltzfus, 2008; Natarajan, 2014).

The tension between real-time diplomacy and diplomacy's need for time was evident on the 22nd of June, 2015, when a United Nations Independent Commission of Inquiry into the 2014 Gaza Conflict published a report of its findings. The report's publication was first announced by a single tweet on the UN's Human Rights Council Twitter channel. Within one hour of its publication, the report's findings made headlines in news websites in Israel, France, Spain and Australia. Within three hours, NGOs dealing with human rights and Palestinian independence tweeted the commission's findings. Yet 12 hours after the report's publication, no major European MFA commented on it online. It's fair to assume that MFAs were busy studying the report while pooling insight from different departments. This was a complex foreign policy event dealing with the issues of conduct of warfare, the International Criminal Court and the future of the Palestinian-Israeli conflict. Yet this time lag raises the question—how can MFAs impact public opinion and the framing of events when they are the last to comment on them?

The challenges of digital diplomacy surveyed thus far are summarized in the image below.

Recently, scholars have begun to evaluate MFAs' ability to realize the potential, and avoid the pitfalls, of digital diplomacy. The following section includes an overview of such studies.

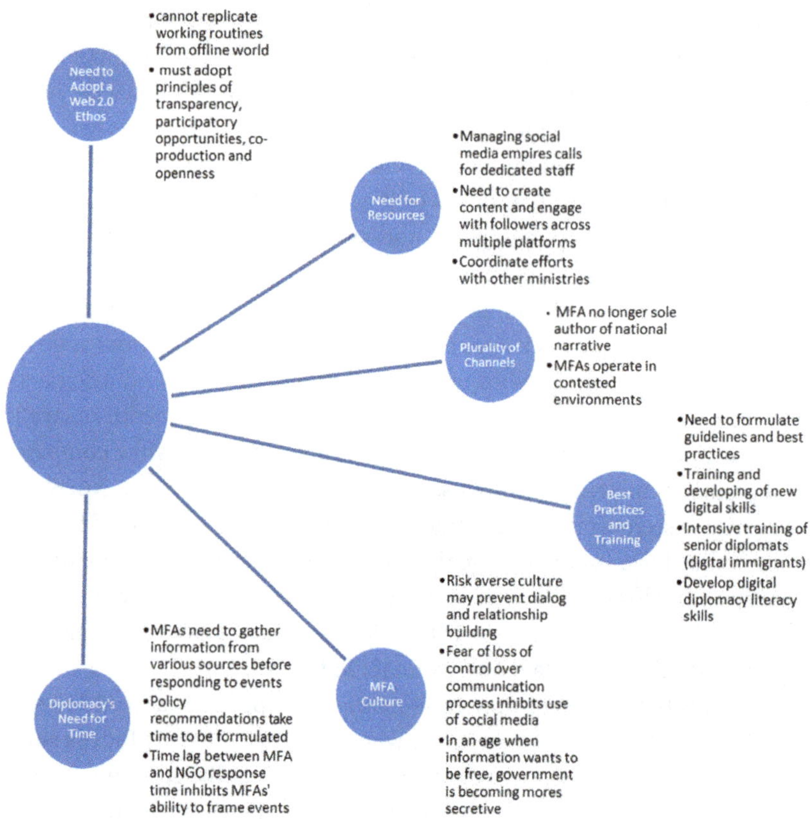

The challenges of digital diplomacy.

Digital Diplomacy: From Theory to Practice

On selfie diplomacy. Manor and Segev (2015) recently evaluated the "selfie" the US state department is projecting to the world via SNS. Content analysis revealed that the US is branding itself as an economically responsible superpower, guided by morals and dedicated to creating a new relationship with the Muslim world. However, this study also highlighted the challenges of selfie diplomacy. As Manor and Segev observe, changing a nation's image is a long-term and intricate process given, that such images serve as stereotypes (Kotler & Gertner, 2002; Papadopoulos & Heslop, 2002). Secondly, the state department is not the only governmental body shaping the US's online selfie. The question that arises is: Does the department coordinate its selfie with other US agencies and ministries?

According to Natarajan (2014), creating a national image includes narrating one's foreign policy goals and depicting the kind of actor they will be in world politics. When exploring India's current narrative of "soft power," Natarajan finds that it focuses on India's rich and diverse democratic culture, thereby resonating with established norms in a Western-influenced world order (Natarajan, 2014). As such, the "soft power" narrative may be demonstrative of Van Ham's social power concept (Van Ham, 2013). Natarajan also found that India's digital diplomacy efforts focus on message dissemination while disregarding the need to counter extremist narratives that, through social media, span the globe.

Khatib, Dutton & Thelwall (2012) explored how the US counters extremist narratives by evaluating the online activity of the US Digital Outreach Team (DOT) in discussion forums following Obama's 2009 Cairo address. Findings indicate that DOT participation in discussions started by private users was minimal. Likewise, DOT seemed to publish identical content across multiple platforms, which focused on pre-determined themes such as US multiculturalism. The analysis revealed two main challenges to the DOT's activity. First, a slow response time to users' comments which inhibits the ability to practice dialogue. Secondly, negative stances towards the US only intensified following DOT posts, possibly due to the fact that the DOT interacts with users who already hold negative views of America. Khatib, Dutton & Thelwall argue that the DOT's activity does demonstrate the ability to stimulate online conversations while also possibly winning over "lurkers" who visit web forums yet do not take an active part in discussions.

Practicing dialogue. The theoretical foundation of digital diplomacy rests on its ability to foster two-way interaction as a means of creating relationships with foreign populations. However, the current research corpus indicates that embassies and MFAs rarely practice public engagement on social media. While exploring public engagement at the embassy level, Vance (2012) interviewed US diplomats formally stationed in Eastern Europe. Interviewees stated that public engagement was best practiced through traditional mass media, which reach vast audiences, and face-to-face engagement in the form of visits to companies or schools. Diplomats further argued that relationships can only be formed in face-to-face opportunities. These results suggest that diplomats may resist new technologies, as they seem to prefer established working routines and lack confidence in technology.

Conversely, in her interviews with foreign diplomats stationed in London, Archetti (2012) found that embassies have adopted new technologies given the greater impact ICT's have had on diplomacy. New technologies have challenged the representational and informational faculties of embassies because world leaders and MFAs now communicate directly with one another and capitals can directly monitor events in foreign countries. In the hope of counter-balancing this loss, embassies have invested greater resources in public diplomacy activities, including engagement through new technologies.

By analyzing the digital diplomacy activity of foreign embassies to China, Bjola and Jiang (2015) found that embassies routinely use social media to communicate with online publics. However, while embassies used SNS to determine which issues would be discussed with followers, this study found little evidence of actual two-way interaction, as embassies did not respond to followers' queries nor did they respond to posts in which they were tagged. The study also found that embassies follow elites rather than ordinary citizens, thus limiting their ability to listen to foreign publics. These results are in line with Fisher's (2010) claim that public diplomacy practitioners use social media for message dissemination rather than relationship building. Similarly, Cha, Yeo & Kim (2015) found that foreign embassies to South Korea are passive in their communication with followers due to budgetary restrictions.

Clarke (2015) evaluated whether MFAs' use of social media has brought with it a departure from the status quo, given the adoption of new norms and problem solving techniques. Analyzing tweets published by the British and Canadian MFAs, Clarke found that Twitter serves as a tool for top-down, state-centric, one-way communication rather than a platform for collaboration with non-state actors. MFAs mostly re-tweet information provided by internal departments or other ministries. Thus, while MFA communication has become networked, the network is still state-centric.

Networked and collaborative approaches to diplomacy. Park and Lim (2014) examined the information networks of Korean and Japanese public diplomacy organizations as a means of investigating the practice of networked diplomacy. The public diplomacy organizations sampled were managed by ministries, agencies and NGOs all dedicated to promoting Japanese and Korean cultures. Employing network and content analysis, the researchers found that the majority of public diplomacy organizations were linked to one another, thus creating dense interconnected networks. However, while Korean organizations were found to be conversational (i.e., posing questions to followers), Japanese organization focused on message dissemination.

Kamp, Manor & Segev (2015) employed Kent & Taylor's (1998) framework for dialogic communication in order to investigate whether MFAs practice dialogic and collaborative public diplomacy. Using a sample of 11 MFAs, the authors evaluated content shared on Twitter and Facebook as well as the adoption of a web 2.0 ethos. Results of a six-week analysis suggest that actual engagement between MFAs and SNS followers is rare. When engagement did occur, it was in the form of Q&A sessions dedicated to a sole issue. This study suggests that MFAs have yet to adopt web 2.0 principles such as participatory opportunities, co-production and collaboration. Thus, the researchers conclude that MFAs have largely failed to realize the dialogic and collaborative potential of social media.

Overcoming the limitations of traditional diplomacy. While digital diplomacy offers the ability to overcome the limitations of traditional diplomacy, two recent case studies illustrate the difficulty of using such platforms for public engagement.

As part of its nation branding activities, in 2007 Sweden opened an online embassy in the virtual world of Second Life. Named the Second House of Sweden, this embassy was meant to facilitate direct engagement with Second Life users, thus reaching a global audience while showcasing Swedish art and culture. The embassy hosted lectures on Swedish culture, organized concerts and celebrated Sweden's national day. According to Pamment (2013), the embassy focused on providing visitors with unique experiences rather than simply disseminating information. However, the embassy was met with criticism, as it was seen as a state-sponsored invasion of Second Life. Likewise, events failed to attract mass audiences. While the embassy closed after five years, Pamment asserts that it demonstrated the need to transition from information-based public diplomacy to activity-based public diplomacy in virtual places. Thus, it may have been a precursor of dialogic diplomacy practiced via social media.

In 2011, the US launched Virtual Embassy Tehran which offered many of the services of a brick-and-mortar embassy, including information on US policies, study opportunities in the US and visa applications. One of the stated goals of the virtual embassy was to leverage interaction with Iranians in order to increase pressure on the Iranian regime. However, Metzgar (2012) found little evidence of actual two-way engagement, stating that the site mainly served as a one-way information hub used to debunk myths about the US. However, Metzgar also states that Virtual Embassy Tehran enabled the US to create an image that counters that of the "great devil," to build its soft power resources in Iran and to communicate with tech-savvy Iranians able to circumvent government censorship of the site.

Critiquing dialogue. The studies reviewed thus far suggest that MFAs use social media to disseminate information and practice monologic, rather than dialogic, public diplomacy. However, Zhang (2013) argues that the concept of symmetrical communication should not be limited to dialogue. Recent alterations to Grunig and Hunt's (1984) symmetrical model of communication suggest that organizations try to meet their own objectives while at the same time helping others achieve theirs. Thus, it is possible for organizations and publics to be both competitive and cooperative. Such a "mixed motive" model suggests that two-way symmetrical communication is more than dialogue and is composed of various forms of interactions, including monologue. For instance, Zhang argues that embassies may use social media as a strategic tool to raise awareness of an issue, frame their agenda and negotiate conflicts with the local population. These may be achieved by monologic communication.

The table below identifies which MFAs have been the subject of digital diplomacy studies thus far. Studies that have focused on the embassy level were excluded from this table. As can be seen, the present digital diplomacy research corpus has tended to focus on the activity of the US state department, even though the adoption of social media by MFAs is a truly global phenomenon. Moreover, only a small fraction of studies have focused on the digital diplomacy activity of smaller nations (e.g., Finland, Norway) or that of Eastern European and Middle Eastern MFAs.

TABLE 1 *Foreign ministries evaluated in digital diplomacy studies*

Study	MFAs Evaluated (by country name)	Main Findings
Attias, S. (2012). Israel's new peer-to-peer diplomacy. *The Hague Journal of Diplomacy,* 7(4), 473–482.	Israel	Peer to peer diplomacy represents the latest shift in diplomatic practice as social media enables citizens to collaborate with MFAs on the production and dissemination of government information. The case study of Israel's peer to peer diplomacy highlights the potential, and pitfalls, of MFA-public collaborations.
Causey, C., & Howard, P. N. (2013). Delivering Digital Public Diplomacy. In R. S. Zaharna, A. Arsenault & A. Fisher (Eds.), *Relational, networked and collaborative approaches to public diplomacy: The connective mindshift* (pp. 144–156). Oxon: Routledge.	US	Social media enables MFAs to gather information in real time. Yet it also necessitates they adopt new information sharing practices and transition to more open models of government in which diplomats engage with online publics. Exploring the state department's response to the WikLeaks scandal reveals that it has failed to adopt new information sharing practices and may be transitioning towards even more conservative information management policies.

Study	MFAs Evaluated (by country name)	Main Findings
Clarke, A. (2015). Business as Usual? An evaluation of British and Canadian digital diplomacy as policy change. In C. Bjola and M. Holmes (Eds.), *Digital Diplomacy Theory and Practice* (pp. 111–126). Oxon: Routledge.	United Kingdom, Canada	A review of British and Canadian digital diplomacy activities suggest that Twitter serves as a tool for top-down, state centric, one-way communication rather than a platform for collaboration with non-state actors. Thus, while diplomacy is networked, is remains state centric.
Comor, E. (2013). Digital Engagement: America's Use (and Misuse) of Marshall McLuhan. *New Political Science, 35*(1), 1–18.	US	As part of its adoption of social media, the US state department has eagerly embraced concepts put forth by Marshall McLuhan, namely the "global village" and the "medium is the message". However, the Department's use of these concepts is at odds with its attempts to manage dissent through social media and re-brand America.
Comor, E., & Bean, H. (2012). America's 'engagement' delusion Critiquing a public diplomacy consensus. *International Communication Gazette, 74*(3), 203–220.	US	Although it claims to use social media to promote dialogue with foreign publics, the Obama administration employs digital tools, and the term "engagement", to influence foreign publics into accepting US polices. The authors argue that a more ethical form of social media use is warranted.
Hallams, E. (2010). Digital diplomacy: the internet, the battle for ideas & US foreign policy.	US	The US state department is employing social media and the internet in order to stimulate debate and discussions with the Muslim

TABLE 1 *Foreign ministries evaluated in digital diplomacy studies* (cont.)

Study	MFAs Evaluated (by country name)	Main Findings
CEU Political Science Journal, (04), 538–574.		world thus countering Al-Qaida's online narrative. As such, the use of digital tools is now an important power resource for the US alongside traditional Hard Power resources.
Hayden, C. (2012). Social Media at State: Power, Practice, and Conceptual Limits for US Public Diplomacy. *Global Media Journal-American Edition, 11*(21).	US	Social media serves as a catalyst to re-envision the role and goals of public diplomacy in US foreign policy. Social media may be used in order to adopt networked models of diplomacy that facilitate collaborations with non-state actors and a connected online public. However, while the state department promotes social media use it is still trying to control the discussion thus limiting its networking abilities.
Kampf, R., Manor, I., & Segev, E. (2015). Digital Diplomacy 2.0? A Cross-national Comparison of Public Engagement in Facebook and Twitter. *The Hague Journal of Diplomacy* (Forthcoming)	Ethiopia, India, Israel, Japan, Kenya, Poland, Rwanda, Somalia, South Korea, US and the United Kingdom	Despite the mass migration of MFAs to social media, dialogue and engagement with online publics remains a rare occurrence. When it does occur, engagement is limited to specific issues. As such, MFAs have failed to realize the dialogic potential of social media.
Khatib, L., Dutton, W., & Thelwall, M. (2012). Public Diplomacy 2.0: A Case Study of the US Digital Outreach Team.	US	The scholars evaluated the activity of the state department's Digital Outreach Team (DOT) following President Obama's Cairo address. The DOT's ability to engage in

Study	MFAs Evaluated (by country name)	Main Findings
The Middle East Journal, 66(3), 453–472.		dialogue was found to be limited given a slow response time to comments and the publication of identical content across online platforms. However, the DOT's activity may demonstrate the potential of using social media to alter the perceptions of hostile online audiences through engagement.
Manor, I., & Segev, E. (2015). America's selfie: how the US portrays itself on its social media accounts. In C. Bjola and M. Holmes (Eds.), *Digital Diplomacy Theory and Practice* (pp. 89–108). Oxon: Routledge.	US	The US state department uses social media in order to manage its global image and reputation. Content analysis suggests that the US currently brands itself as an economically responsible superpower, guided by moral values and committed to diplomacy and building meaningful relationships with the Arab and Muslim worlds.
Metzgar, E. T. (2012). Is it the medium or the message? Social media, American public relations & Iran. *Global Media Journal*, 1–16.	US	Virtual Embassy Teheran was launched by the US state department in order to foster dialogue between the US and Iranian citizens. However, Metzgar found little evidence of dialogue suggesting that that embassy serves as a one way information hub used to debunk myths about the US. Yet the Virtual Embassy does demonstrate the internet's potential to overcome limitations of traditional diplomacy and build Soft Power resources.

TABLE 1 *Foreign Ministries Evaluated in Digital Diplomacy Studies* (cont.)

Study	MFAs Evaluated (by country name)	Main Findings
Natarajan, K. (2014). Digital Public Diplomacy and a Strategic Narrative for India. *Strategic Analysis*, *38*(1), 91–106.	India	India's MFA has begun using social media in order to author an Indian national narrative and align India with acceptable norms thus increasing the nation's international legitimacy. However, the ministry has yet to harness social media in order to construct a strategic narrative for India and counter radical narratives that are spread online.
Ociepka, B. (2012). Impact of New Technologies on International Communication: The Case of Public Diplomacy. *Information Science*, (59), 24–36.	Bulgaria, Czech Republic, Estonia, Latvia, Lithuania, Poland, Romania, Slovakia, Slovenia	An exploration of the use of social media by Eastern European MFAs calls into doubt the ability of SNS to foster networked models of diplomacy or advance relational approached to public diplomacy through online dialogue.
Pamment, J. *New Public Diplomacy in the 21st Century*. 2013: Routledge.	Sweden	Sweden's Virtual Embassy in Second Life may have served as a precursor to digital diplomacy as it offered visitors a unique virtual experience. However, the model of a Virtual Embassy ultimately failed as events did not to attract audiences. Likewise, the embassy was seen as a state sponsored invasion of Second Life.
Rana, K., S.(2013). Diaspora Diplomacy and Public Diplomacy. In R. S. Zaharna,	India, Mexico, China, Kenya	Diaspora diplomacy has gained increasing prominence in international relations. MFAs such as India, Mexico, China and Kenya

Study	MFAs Evaluated (by country name)	Main Findings
A. Arsenault & A. Fisher (Eds.), *Relational, networked and collaborative approaches to public diplomacy: The connective mindshift* (pp. 70–85). Oxon: Routledge.		are adopting new policies to maintain, and deepen, their ties with communities of expats. These include cultural events, publications, economic ties, aid during consular crises and social media engagement.
Seo, H. (2013). The "Virtual Last Three Feet". In R. S. Zaharna, A. Arsenault & A. Fisher (Eds.), *Relational, networked and collaborative approaches to public diplomacy: The connective mindshift* (pp. 157–169). Oxon: Routledge.	US	Social media may be used in order to adopt networked models of public diplomacy in which MFAs create trans-national networks through online engagement. The US state department, for instance, is using social media to engage in dialogue with foreign publics in South Korea. This case study reveals that MFAs must take into account the cultural context in which they operate (e.g., Korean culture) and emphasize their commitment to sincere and open engagement.
Stoltzfus, K. (2008). Exploring US e-diplomacy and non-state actors' increasing communicative influence. In *Proceedings of the 2008 international conference on Digital government research* (pp. 347–354).	US	Non-state actors have increasingly asserted their influence in international diplomacy through their ability gather and disseminate information. Governmental partnerships with non-state actors are therefore viewed as beneficial. Through an exploration of the US state department's association with non-state actors this study offers a model for understanding the new information dynamics that impact diplomacy.

TABLE 1 *Foreign Ministries Evaluated in Digital Diplomacy Studies* (cont.)

Study	MFAs Evaluated (by country name)	Main Findings
Stein, J. G. (2011). Introduction. In J. G. Stein (Ed.), *Diplomacy in the Digital Age* (pp. 1–9). Canada: McClelland & Stewart.	Canada	This collective volume explores various aspects of Canada's digital diplomacy activities including: how MFAs may cope with the emergence of an unpredictable and volatile online public, the need to adopt new practices given whole-of-government approaches to diplomacy that challenge an MFA's ability to narrate a coherent national narrative and the use of networks to offer innovative solutions to global challenges.
Vance, A. M. (2012). Post-9/11 US Public Diplomacy in Eastern Europe: Dialogue via New Technologies or Face-to-Face Communication?. *Global Media Journal—American Edition, 11* (21).	US	Interviews with US diplomats previously stationed in Eastern Europe reveal that diplomats still value face-to-face interactions over virtual ones. Interviewees stated that public engagement was best practiced through traditional mass media. This study suggests that established working routines influence diplomats' willingness to adopt new technologies.
Xiguang, L., & Jing, W. (2010). Web-based public diplomacy: The role of social media in the Iranian and Xinjiang riots. *Journal of International Communication, 16*(1), 7–22.	China	Social media has the ability to empower citizens that now constitute a knowledgeable online demos. However, these abilities may also be used by groups to create "smart mobs" that challenge the state. As social media continues to proliferate, its importance in diplomacy grows. Thus, China should adopt social media tools in order to increase its agenda setting and public diplomacy capabilities.

In summary, digital diplomacy studies have consistently shown that MFAs have yet to realize the dialogic potential of SNS. However, these studies have failed to analyze the reason for this or evaluate the manner in which MFAs themselves conceptualize and define online engagement or the goals they wish to achieve through the adoption of SNS. Likewise, digital diplomacy studies have tended to focus solely on diplomatic institutions without examining the impact brought about by the migration of additional governmental ministries and agencies online. Such migration suggests that MFAs are not the sole author of their national image and narrative. The incorporation of SNS by MFAs must therefore be analyzed through a wider prism, especially in the age of whole-of-government approaches to diplomacy (Golberg & Kaduck, 2011).

Moreover, the studies reviewed in this section tend to focus on either digital diplomacy at the embassy level or the MFA level. Yet the practice of digital diplomacy involves continued cooperation and information sharing between MFAs and their embassies. The adoption of new technologies necessitates these be institutionalized through the development of working routines, guidelines and employee training. This aspect has received little attention by academic scholars. Likewise, few studies have shed light on the practitioners of digital diplomacy at both the MFA and embassy level. Is digital diplomacy the domain of career diplomats, who are able to narrate foreign policy? Or is it the domain of communications and social media experts, who are able to author attractive online content? Should it be the former, MFAs may be unable to communicate with large audiences. Should it be the latter, the medium may become more important than the message. The identity of these practitioners therefore directly impacts the practice of digital diplomacy and MFAs' ability to reap the benefits of migrating online.

Finally, most studies tend to assume that all MFAs practice and conceptualize digital diplomacy in the same manner. Thus, studies offer insights and solutions that follow the rationale of "one size fits all." However, one should expect a certain degree of variance in the practice of digital diplomacy. Some MFAs, for instance, began their migration online more than two decade ago (e.g., Sweden), while others have just recently ventured online (e.g., Iran). The longer an MFA has been online, the more likely it is to have developed guidelines and best practices for diplomats. Organizational culture may also vary and impact the use of social media by MFAs. Centralized and bureaucratic MFAs may inhibit diplomats' online activity, given their need to gain approval of content published online. Such a culture also inhibits the practice of real-time diplomacy (Seib, 2012). On the other hand, for MFAs in which power has migrated to the embassies, diplomats may demonstrate more initiative—thus leading to the adoption of new approaches and tools in the practice of digital diplomacy.

Even an MFA's standing in government may bring about variance in the practice of digital diplomacy. In Israel, for instance, an abundance of ministries deal with foreign affairs. Such a state of affairs brings about a need to coordinate online activity with a multitude of actors. Despite growing interest in digital diplomacy, few studies to date have attempted to explore and explain such variance. This is the ultimate goal of this study. The following section details the research question and methodology employed in order to meet this important goal.

Research Questions and Methodology

This study aims to understand how MFAs vary in their use of social media and to explain such variances. Variance in the use of social media was explored by the extent to which MFAs have been able to realize the potential of digital diplomacy by a) institutionalizing the use of social media in their organizations; b) reaping the benefits of social media; and c) overcoming the challenges of migrating to social media.

The question of institutionalizing digital diplomacy warrants further elaboration. It is the view of the researcher that using digital tools such as social media and SNS does not in itself indicate that MFAs have institutionalized digital diplomacy. Rather, institutionalizing digital diplomacy is understood as a process through which an organization has developed the capacity to use such tools in order to achieved diplomatic goals. This includes but is not limited to: developing guidelines and articulating best practices to guide diplomats migrating online; offering training for junior and senior diplomats and relinquishing control over the communication process as a pre-requisite for MFA-public engagement. This suggests that MFAs may vary in the extent to which they have institutionalized digital diplomacy. It is this variation that demonstrates the manner in which an analysis of MFAs' ability to realize the potential of digital diplomacy answers this study's over-reaching question of how MFAs vary in their use of social media.

According to Alexander Wednt (1998), one approach to international relations has the goal of finding causal mechanisms. Wendt states that causal theories have become associated with positivist approaches to IR. Another approach, associated with post-positivists and referred to as constitutive theories, has the goal of recovering the "individual and shared meanings that motivated actors to do what they did" (Wendt, 1998, p. 102). Although Wendt calls on IR scholars to adopt both approaches, he differentiates between causal and constitutive theories by the questions they ask. Causal theories ask "Why" questions while constitutive theories ask "How-Possible" or "What" questions. Constitutive questions are such that aim to uncover why a certain system is constituted and operates the way it does. This is achieved by searching for an insider's look into the system and the agents that constitute it (Wendt, 1998).

The theoretical perspective of this study rests on Wendt's (1998) constitutive approach to international relations. As such, this article does not offer a causal explanation to the practice of digital diplomacy, but rather it explores its practice through the prism of diplomats. There are several reasons for the adoption of a constitutive approach in this study. First, the topic of analysis is a social one since diplomacy is a social institution (Hocking & Melissen, 2015) managed by social beings (i.e., diplomats) and constituted on ideas. Secondly, before digital diplomacy may be practiced and mastered, it must first be imagined by diplomats. Third, digital diplomacy is not a "stable" phenomenon (Wendt, 1998) but a dynamic and ever-changing practice.

Finally, there was no one occurrence that led to the emergence of digital diplomacy. Indeed, there were myriad occurrences, actors and processes that ultimately led diplomats and their institutions to migrate online. As such, when these events came into being, digital diplomacy came into being with them. Digital diplomacy was and is constituted through interaction within MFAs, between MFAs, between MFAs and the public, and between MFAs and other institutions (e.g., government ministries, NGOs).

Given that the realization of the potential of digital diplomacy rests on three pillars, each pillar was translated into a research question.

RQ1: Have MFAs institutionalized digital diplomacy?

RQ2: Have MFAs reaped the benefits of digital diplomacy?

RQ3: Have MFAs overcome the challenges of digital diplomacy?

Methodology

Sample. This study explored the digital diplomacy model of the Finnish, Israeli, Norwegian and Polish MFAs. These were selected out of a desire to evaluate mid-sized MFAs that may have eagerly adopted digital diplomacy because of its cost-effectiveness and its ability to increase the visibility of MFAs among news outlets and the diplomatic milieu. The MFAs also constitute a homogenous study sample with regard to Western culture, SNS penetration, GDP and location along the digital divide. Such homogeneity enables a comparison between these four MFAs as well as the possible generalization of the study's findings with regard to mid-sized Western MFAs. Finally, only two of these ministries have been evaluated in previous studies (e.g., Israel and Poland). Thus, this study contributes to the digital diplomacy research corpus by expanding its reach.

The foreign ministries that participated in this study were contacted by email or direct messages on Twitter and asked if they would partake in a comparative study. The study's abstract was then sent to each MFA. Initially, six MFAs were approached, but two declined to participate in the study.

Measures

RQ1: Have MFAs institutionalized digital diplomacy? This question was answered by evaluating the manner in which MFAs train diplomats in the use of social media and the existence of best practices and guidelines to guide diplomats. In addition, the manner in which MFAs supervise the authoring of social media content at both MFA and embassy level was evaluated. Finally, working routines at both MFA and embassy levels were evaluated with regard to use of SNS for specific activities (e.g., nation branding) and the definition of audiences to be targeted on each SNS (e.g., Twitter, Facebook).

RQ2: Have MFAs reaped the benefits of digital diplomacy Answering this question was achieved by evaluating the manner in which MFAs define and conceptualize public engagement; audiences targeted in nation branding and public diplomacy activities (e.g., newsroom elite, foreign populations, NGOs and civil society; diaspora, local population); parameters used by MFAS to evaluate public diplomacy activity (e.g., re-tweets, number of followers, comments); use of SNS as an information source at both MFA and embassy levels; tailoring of SNS content to local audiences (e.g., language, values, culture), and autonomy of embassy staffers in authoring online content.

RQ3: Have MFAs overcome the challenges of digital diplomacy Answering this question was achieved by evaluating the scope of MFA and embassy online activity (e.g., number of channels and platforms); working routines used to accommodate a 24-hour news cycle; embassy autonomy in responding to real-time events; coordination of MFA social media activity with other ministries and organizations; organization-wide collaboration on the creation of online content; creation of collaborative opportunities and willingness to engage in dialogue with followers and critics.

Procedure. Analyzing MFAs' digital diplomacy models was achieved by a two-step process. First, directors of digital diplomacy units were interviewed over Skype (or face-to-face, in Israel's case). Interviews are a basic method of gathering a rich and in-depth experiential account from respondents (Fontana & Fray, 1994; Whiting, 2007).

The methodology of this study is influenced by its theoretical perspective. Given its constitutive approach, this study views digital diplomacy as a concept conceived and, in turn, practiced by social agents. As such, evaluating the practice of digital diplomacy necessitates a methodological approach that enables one to understand how diplomats define and envision digital diplomacy as a whole, and its advantages and limitations in particular. Therefore, this study employed semi-structured interviews that lasted between 40–60 minutes. As opposed to structured interviews, which explain behaviors along pre-defined categories, semi-structured interviews attempt to understand complex behaviors through a more open conversation in which topics arise from the informants' answers (Fontana & Frey, 1994; Whiting, 2007). Semi-structured interviews enable the informant to more freely express his thoughts while allowing the researcher to grasp the informants' world through his use of language (Al-Saggaf & Williamson, 2004). In such interviews, all respondents are asked identical questions within a flexible framework, allowing the researcher to delve more deeply into specific issues (Britten, 1995; Dearnley, 2005). The interview guide (see Appendix 2) was first employed while interviewing the director of Israel's digital diplomacy unit. Following this interview, several questions were added to the guide so as to better address all three research questions. The final guide was used during interviews with all other participants (see Appendix 3).

Secondly, a questionnaire was completed by an MFA level digital diplomacy staffer. These questionnaires (see Appendix 4) were similar to the interview guide yet included different phrasing and examples so as to elicit in-depth answers in the absence of an interviewer.

Given limited resources, evaluating embassy level digital diplomacy was achieved through the use of a written questionnaire (see Appendix 5) disseminated to embassy level digital diplomacy staffers. Each participating MFA was asked to select five embassies that would participate in the study, the only requirement being that the embassies operate SNS channels. Questionnaires were composed of questions that were similar to the interview guide. However, these included examples and leading questions in order to ensure participants understood each questions despite the absence of interviewers. In total, 20 questionnaires were collected. Similar to the interviews, questionnaires were chosen as a methodological tool to explore the unique prism of the practitioners of digital diplomacy.

It should be noted that each question or group of questions in the questionnaires corresponded with one of the study's research questions. For instance, in the questionnaire disseminated to MFA level digital diplomacy staffers (see Appendix 4), questions 1–8 explored MFA supervision models of content shared online, a definition of audiences, and the use of best practices and guidelines, thus corresponding with RQ1. Questions 9–12, 16–20 and 22–23 dealt with MFA-to-public engagement, the use of SNS as an information source, parameters for evaluating social media activity, and an explanation of how content is tailored to specific audiences, thus corresponding with RQ2. Finally, questions 13–15,

21 and 24 dealt with the number of social media platforms used by the MFAs, coordination of content with other ministries, and the use of SNS to interact with online critics, thus corresponding with RQ3.

Similarly, in the questionnaire disseminated to embassy level digital diplomacy staffers (see Appendix 5), questions 1–4, 15 and 20–21 corresponded with RQ1, questions 8–12, 14 and 18–19 corresponded with RQ2, and questions 5–7, 13 and 17 corresponded with RQ3.

The following section includes the results obtained from interviews and questionnaires. Each analysis begins with an overview of the structure of the digital diplomacy unit and the manner in which the MFA works alongside its embassies. Next, following Bjola and Holmes's definition of digital diplomacy (2015), results are organized in three sections: information dissemination; information gathering; and public diplomacy and nation branding. In order to maintain consistency, embassy level staffers who oversee social media activity are referred to as "digital diplomacy managers."

Results

Poland's MFA

Interview with Agnieszka Skieterska, head of Digital Communication Division. Polish embassies that participated in the study: London, Santiago, Washington, Paris and Vienna.

Structure of Digital Diplomacy Unit

The press-spokesman's office is composed of three elements. The first is the Digital Communication Division, which includes five employees and oversees digital diplomacy activity at the MFA and embassy level. The second is the Promotional Website Unit, which includes three employees and is in charge of promoting Poland abroad. The third is the Media Relations Division, which consists of eight employees and deals with traditional media. Together with the spokesman, the office maintains a staff of 17 employees. In total, the Polish MFA's online presence includes 150 Twitter accounts, 74 Facebook pages, 38 YouTube channels, a Weibo account and a blog.

The Digital Communication Division is headed by Agnieszka Skieterska, a former journalist and social media expert. The Digital Communication Division and the Promotional Website Unit are both also composed of social media experts, former journalists and public relations professionals rather than trained diplomats. These staffers are mostly between the ages of 20 to 30, and are thus digital natives.

Working Alongside Embassies

The MFA's Digital Communication Division supervises and supports the digital diplomacy activity of Polish embassies throughout the world. According to Skieterska, working alongside embassies is a three-step process that includes training, supervision and encouragement. As of 2012, all Polish diplomats posted abroad are required to partake in a three-day social media training course in which they are introduced to SNS and are given practical tools for social media activity such as an understanding of what content is most attractive to SNS users, how to edit information on embassy websites and how to convey foreign policy issues in narrative form for a blog. Online training is also offered to embassy level digital diplomacy managers.

> *We are trying to give them a solid base because while many of them might have Facebook account... it's private. An official one* (account) *is a different thing... training is strongly connected with supervision because it's easier to teach people and then expect something than expect something without giving them* (diplomats) *tools and knowledge.*

Each staff member in the Digital Communication Division and Promotional Website Unit personally supervises the online activity of 15 diplomatic missions in one geographic region (e.g., Baltic states). This includes monitoring the relevance and accuracy of information posted on SNS and websites as well as the quality of multimedia (e.g., videos, images). With the exception of information sent to them by the MFA, embassy level managers have autonomy regarding what information to publish online. However, they do require authorization from the ambassador.

> *We send the local editors articles and facts that they can use on the website but the final decisions lies with the Ambassador if it will be published... sometimes we send things about democratization and that's not always wise to publish... these are sensitive issues.*

In addition, once a year all Polish diplomatic posts are evaluated by the MFA. As part of this evaluation, the posts' digital diplomacy activity is also assessed.

The press office actively encourages diplomats to migrate online. Once a year, the MFA's spokesperson addresses a conference of all Polish ambassadors convened in Warsaw. The department uses this address to motivate ambassadors to migrate online by conveying the importance of a social media presence. As ambassadors approve social media content at the embassy level, it is vital that they understand its importance to the MFA's activities. Embassies may also apply for a social media budget allocated at the discretion of the press office. Such budgets may be used for embassy initiated social media campaigns. Best practices are developed through the weekly publication of "Tweets of the Week," a newsletter that includes the best tweets published by Polish missions around the world.

Information Dissemination

Authoring of online content at MFA level. There is a clear dichotomy in SNS use at the Polish MFA, as Facebook is used solely to promote the Polska brand through the publication of Poland's cultural, economic and scientific achievements. Thus, it is managed by the Promotional Website Unit whose members author all content. Other SNS (e.g., Twitter and YouTube) are all used for public diplomacy activities and are managed by the Digital Communication Division (e.g., diaspora relations, consular activity). Members of the Media Relations Division also tweet on SNS channels during weekend shifts, which due to limited resources are shared by all the press office staffers, as well as live tweeting from media events.

Issues to be addressed online by MFA. Issues to be addressed online are decided upon in meetings between the press spokesman office and heads of the Digital Communication Division and Promotional Websites Unit. In these meetings, the itinerary of the minister and secretaries are reviewed in a search for online content. Issues also include special projects. During such projects, the Digital Communication Division will cooperate with a certain ministerial department in order to promote a major event (e.g., Polish diaspora day). Such routine meetings may be viewed as a tool for ensuring consistency across all MFA channels and the authoring of a coherent national narrative thus overcoming the challenges of plurality of channels.

MFA departments may suggest online content yet the content itself is authored by Digital Communication Division and Promotional Websites Unit staffers. This relationship offers important benefits as career diplomats identify relevant content, thus providing their expertise, while social media experts author the content in a manner that attracts SNS followers. Press office staffers are also welcome to propose content, which must be authorized by the head of the division.

Plurality of online channels. Interestingly, this was not viewed as a major challenge by Skieterska. In fact, she stated that there was a lack of official Polish social media accounts in English.

> *I would even say there is a lack of English information sources… prime minister and president's accounts are only in Polish… we at the MFA regret*

that they are not tweeting in English because it would be good for us to re-tweet them.

The lack of official English language sources was identified by Skieterska as a strain on resources, given that the MFA has to translate Polish language content and author all official Polish social media content in English. Skieterska also stated that her division has informal meetings with the prime minister's social media team, which is very active online. Such meetings may also be viewed as a tool for narrative coordination.

Authoring of online content at the embassy level. The identity of embassy level digital diplomacy managers varies greatly between Polish missions. In embassies with larger staffs, online content may be authored by the spokesman or public diplomacy expert. In smaller embassies, the author is usually a local employee. According to Skieterska, at times it is preferable to have a local employee author online content given the need to communicate in local languages.

This variation was demonstrated in the study sample, as in London the digital diplomacy manager is a 23-year-old local employee who reports to the Public Diplomacy and Communications department, while in Santiago the manager is the 46-year-old husband of a Polish diplomat who reports directly to the ambassador and in Vienna the manager is a 29-year-old career diplomat. Overall, four of the five embassy level managers were digital natives in their early 30s, while one was a digital immigrant. Only two of the five managers were career diplomats.

All embassy digital diplomacy managers expressed their autonomy with regard to content published online. The London manager wrote:

The decision on topics in tweets and Facebook posts is made largely by me and a colleague who shares my responsibilities... though the decision to publicise some events is passed down to me by my supervisor or the ambassador... occasionally we also get instructions from the ministry.

Issues to be addressed online by embassies. When asked what percentage of digital diplomacy content was dictated by the ministry, respondents answered that between 5% to 10% of content published online (i.e., SNS and websites) originated from the ministry. As the Paris digital diplomacy manager wrote:

The general idea is that all employees at the embassy, and diplomats in particular, should contribute by providing interesting news/articles/etc. from their areas of expertise... In practice, I am responsible for 90% of our tweets—from research and formulation to creation of visuals.

This highlights the importance of collaboration between digital diplomacy managers and other embassy departments. Three of the five respondents stated that they "rarely" receive information from other departments. Only two of the five managers partook in embassy meetings in which they may receive information from other departments.

There was a generational gap in the manner in which embassy mangers searched for relevant information to publish online. When asked, "How do you know what topics are regarded as a priority by the ministry?" three digital natives replied that they review the MFA's SNS accounts. Thus, the MFA's Twitter channel becomes an information guide for embassy managers. The digital immigrant, on the other hand, stated:

> *The priorities of the MFA are presented annually by the minister. Moreover, the office of the spokesperson indicates topics.*

Although they enjoy autonomy, there are instances in which the MFA coordinates global social media events that include all diplomatic missions. In May of 2015, embassies throughout the world published information on how Poles traveling abroad may register and vote online in the presidential elections. Consular assistance was also offered via embassy SNS accounts during the Nepal earthquake.

Information Gathering

Information gathering at MFA level. In her interview, Skieterska stated that utilizing SNS as an information source has yet to be implemented at the MFA and embassy levels. When asked if her staffers relay information gathered on Twitter to specific departments in the MFA, she answered:

> *Sometimes political issues that are visible on Twitter and Facebook are posted by us to the relevant departments but it's not very common.*

One example that was discussed at length was the MFA's consular activity during the recent presidential elections, as many Poles tweeted questions regarding an online voting system. Such questions were directed to the relevant department in the MFA.

Embassies have also yet to realize the potential of SNS as a source of information for the MFA. Commenting on embassies' information gathering, Skieterska stated:

> *Sometimes it happens but it's the beginning of the process... some diplomats still don't view social media as an important source of information even if it is... There are posts who are observing and sending so it depends on local mentality at the embassy. It happens but not often.*

These comments raise an important question regarding Poland's digital diplomacy model. As ambassadors oversee digital diplomacy activity, an embassy's online activity depends greatly on the ambassador's belief in social media as a communication and information gathering tool. According to Skieterska, ambassadors are still in a transitional period in which social media is being treated with caution and suspicion.

When asked if the spokesman's department follows other MFAs' social media accounts in order to gather information, Skieterska stated that:

> *We observe other accounts... we are following very closely Russian and Ukrainian accounts due to the situation in Ukraine... it's good to know what they* (Russia & Ukraine) *are thinking about and what is their official line... It is an important source of information. Also, it is a source of inspiration...*

According to Skieterska, her division often reviews other MFAs' activity in order to better their practice of digital diplomacy and integrate new ideas and tools.

Information gathering at embassy level. In order to evaluate the flow of information from embassies to the MFA, embassy managers were asked how often they communicate with the MFA, and to what purpose. Respondents answered that they communicate with the ministry between once and twice a month. However, such communication seems to be limited to technical assistance. No embassy manager raised the issue of relaying information gathered from local SNS and online conversations to the MFA.

Public Diplomacy and Nation Branding

Nation branding at MFA level. The Promotional Websites Unit publishes content that highlights Polish cultural achievements and historic milestones. Such content is published solely on Facebook and designated websites. Content is curated by the head of the unit, who also supervises content published by staffers.

Public diplomacy at MFA level. The MFA's Polish language SNS accounts target the domestic population, while its English accounts are targeted mainly at opinion makers, journalists, diplomats and politicians. Skieterska did later add another important audience—foreign populations. She also noted the importance of *influencing* them in order to achieve foreign policy goals. The spokesman's office routinely analyzes its social media audience in order to learn if it has attracted Polish media outlets, foreign MFAs and foreign missions in Poland. The importance assigned to MFAs and diplomats stationed in Poland may be representative of a network mentality. The MFA also operates a Polish language Twitter channel that deals solely with consular aid.

Public engagement at MFA level. While the Digital Communication Division and Promotional Website Unit have separate mandates (e.g., public diplomacy, nation branding) both deal with the issue of engagement with online followers. When asked to define the term "engagement," Skieterska stated:

> *From our point of view engagement is mostly sharing the information.*

When asked about engaging in dialogue with SNS followers, Skieterska referred to the MFA's cautious mentality toward social media:

> *Engagement, of course, is important, but we are not active enough... because for years we were trying to relate the importance of it* (engagement) *to senior officials... engaging followers is something new... we are aware it has to be an important part of our communication.*

However, she also stressed the fact that engagement is also rare on the part of social media followers. Her experience suggests that the majority of followers are not keen on engaging with MFAs on issues of shared concern:

> *I'm quite surprised, because I must say that we are not receiving a lot of questions from citizens... We will not reply to social media hate... But, we don't receive a lot of real questions... Mostly people criticize the political part of our job and we will not discuss this because you cannot discuss with someone who hates the country.*

This quote not only conveys the division's sense that followers aren't keen on engagement, but also states that as a matter of policy the Polish MFA does not engage in dialogue with critics of Poland, with one important exception: "*misinterpretation of history concerning German Nazi concentration camps on the territory of occupied Poland during the Second World War.*"

Measuring public engagement at MFA level. The MFA evaluates its public engagement through two parameters: reach of content (e.g., re-tweets, number of followers) and comments posted by followers. This is achieved by utilizing free diagnostic tools (e.g., Twitter analytics). Scope of dialogue is not measured.

One of the major challenges facing the MFA is growing competition over social media followers as other MFAs are also active online. According to Skieterska, this necessitates growing resources in order to train staffers, accommodate a 24-hour news cycle, remain active on weekends and offer followers better-prepared content.

Between public diplomacy and nation branding. The Polish MFA and its embassies spend resources altering the historic perception of Poland's involvement in Nazi atrocities during World War Two. This is manifest in monitoring news articles about Nazi atrocities and insisting on the term "Nazi camps in occupied Poland" rather than "Polish Death Camps." Such is the case in the tweet shown below that was published by the Polish embassy in Ireland.

In addition to such corrections, MFA staffers will correct SNS followers who are using the term "Polish camps" or misrepresenting Poland's role in the war. There is also a Twitter channel dedicated to this issue (@GermanNaziCamps).

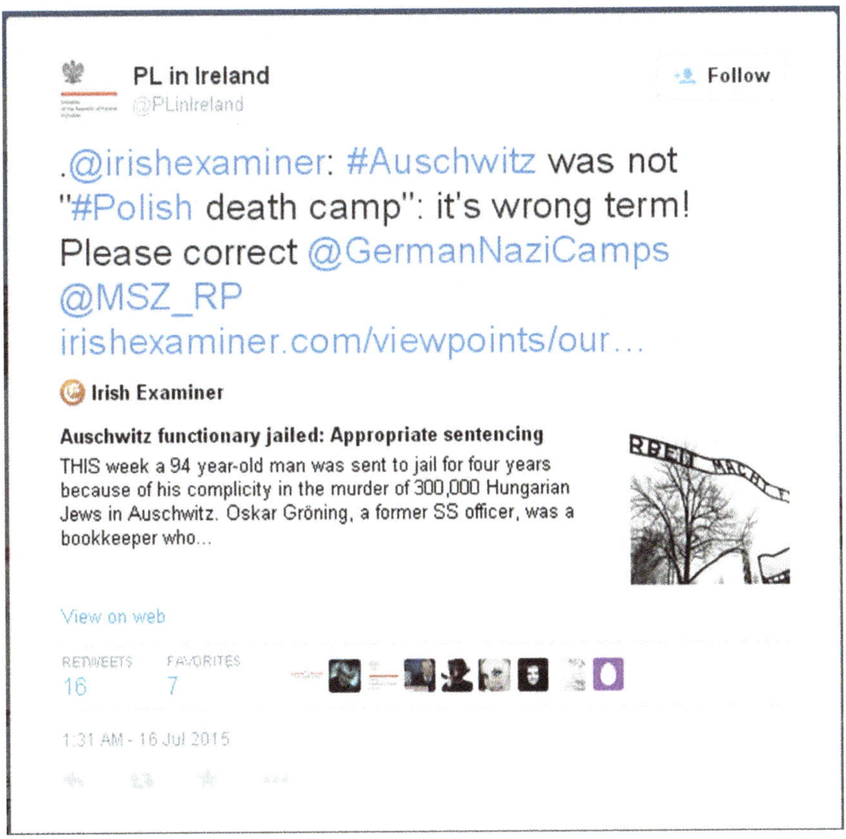

However, before engaging with followers on this or any other issue, staffers must request authorization from their superior. The MFA's activity regarding its history seems to relate to both Poland's image and its conversations with global audiences.

Public diplomacy and nation branding at embassy level. The embassy managers oversee both public diplomacy and nation branding activities. Polish embassies target four online audiences: the local population, the diplomatic corps, Polish domestic audiences and the Polish MFA that re-tweets information posted by its embassies. This necessitates that managers publish content in the local language, English (for the diplomatic corps) and Polish. The dichotomy of using Facebook for nation branding activities and Twitter for public diplomacy goals was evident among all embassy managers thus demonstrating the MFA's ability to institute working routines throughout the organization. As the manager in Vienna wrote:

> *The main criterion on Twitter is to anticipate, communicate or create upcoming or "breaking" news… therefore we are on Twitter 24/7. The main criterion on Facebook is to present ourselves as an up to date institution which represents Poland in Austria.*

Public engagement at embassy level. When asked to define "engagement," the majority of respondents stated that it deals with issues of information dissemination without mentioning dialogue. However, there was a generational gap in which digital natives included components reflecting a web 2.0 ethos. A 33-year-old manager defined it as:

> *Listen. Inform. Interact. Be transparent and responsive.*

Another manager, aged 35, defined engagement as:

> *A more open, direct and democratic way of communicating with people/ users rather than just governments and institutions.*

The digital immigrant, on the other hand, saw engagement as:

> *Informing and distributing news about my country, activities of our embassy and MFA, creating a good image of Poland and Polish people.*

When asked if the MFA stresses the need to engage with online followers, answers varied substantially from "*not at all*" to "*a very strong emphasis.*"

When asked who their target audience was, embassy managers mentioned the local population and *influencers*, in particular politicians and opinion leaders (e.g., journalists, bloggers, members of the academic community). These definitions seem to place an emphasis on elites rather than the local citizenry. However, two embassy managers stated that they mostly engage with the Polish diaspora on consular issues.

Interestingly, all embassy digital diplomacy managers stated that they do not engage with critics of Poland demonstrating the possible effectiveness of the MFA in instituting an organization-wide policy. When asked if the MFA emphasizes or forbids engagement with critics, one manager answered:

> *I personally tend to avoid interacting with trolls because it is an entirely futile exercise.*

Measuring public engagement at embassy level. Embassy managers all stated that they routinely evaluate their public diplomacy activity. This includes identifying their actual audience base through the use of SNS analytical tools and using parameters to evaluate reach of content (e.g., shares, re-tweets). Only one manager stated that she attempts to create content based on the interests of her audience, a form of tailoring.

> *I try to analyze our audience base on a regular basis—this concerns not only the number of followers, who they are, where they are from, and what information might interest them.*

However, when asked if they re-phrase MFA tweets or simply re-tweet them, the majority of respondents answered the latter adding that they simply translate MFA tweets to local languages. Finally, all embassy managers stated that they use feedback from followers (e.g., number of "Likes," favorites) to develop best practices, create more attractive content and identify which content best suits each medium.

Summary

The Polish MFA's digital diplomacy model includes close supervision of online content published at the MFA and embassy level. While supervision may prevent faux pas, it may also limit the MFA's ability to react in real time to events taking place, as well as inhibit embassies' ability to converse with online followers. The Polish MFA's rigorous supervision model may therefore prevent the MFA and embassies from fully reaping the benefits of social media use. Notably, supervision models were not originally envisioned by the researcher as a factor that influences MFA digital diplomacy activity. Given its emphasis on training and supervision, the Polish digital diplomacy model may be characterized as "train and supervise." As the press office coordinates all nation branding and public diplomacy content published online, the MFA may be able to narrate a coherent foreign policy and national image. Surprisingly, the majority of Polish embassies do not seem to collaborate on the production of online content, thus limiting the amount of information the embassy level manager may publish which, in turn, limits online engagement with followers. The fact that Polish embassies publish content in Polish, English and local languages demonstrates a network mentality in which an online embassy belongs to a myriad of social networks. Results suggest that both the Polish MFA and its embassies have yet to utilize SNS as information gathering tools, a finding that contradicts previous scholarly work. Finally, most evaluation parameters focus on information dissemination rather than dialogue.

Finland's MFA

Interview with Olli Moilanen, head of web communications. Embassies that participated in the study: London, Paris, Washington, Beijing and Tokyo.

Structure of Digital Diplomacy Unit

There is no digital diplomacy unit in the Finnish MFA. This is reflective of the ministry's belief that the digital age has not brought with it a new form of diplomacy but, rather, that digital tools have impacted the practice of diplomacy. As one MFA staffer stated:

> *If you start talking about "digital diplomacy" it's as if it's a separate thing—it's not. It's an extension of what we do. The digitalization has changed how we do it. Diplomacy in the digital age could be more useful in addressing both communications and larger topics, such as digitalization, cybersecurity.*

The communications department at the MFA is in charge of both traditional and social media activities. The department is made up of four units. The Public Diplomacy unit, which is headed by a career diplomat, is tasked with social media use mainly for the purpose of nation branding activities. The MFA's nation branding activities are all part of the "This is Finland" campaign, which includes the Finland.fl web portal, Twitter channels, Facebook profiles, YouTube and Weibo accounts. According to the head of web communications, Olli Moilanen, the Finnish MFA still values websites, and its activities therefore include a myriad of SNS profiles and web portals.

Working Alongside Embassies

All diplomats to be stationed abroad partake in a social media training course prior to their departure. The course focuses on acquainting diplomats with social media tools and offering practical guidance on how to use SNS. While most training takes place at the ministry, the MFA offers remote training to embassy digital diplomacy managers. The ministry encourages its diplomats to be active on social media. Currently, the communications department is laboring on a new program that will offer more social media support to diplomats thus facilitating their migration online.

> *We cannot do it for them.... we can encourage and give support... the goal is to make sure that in the digital world, Finland is visible and networks are built... like in traditional diplomacy you need to get information from your networks and influence your networks.*

In addition, the ministry creates and disseminates content to its embassies.

> *Units of the communications department are in daily contact with embassies... Materials for global use in social media are provided to the embassies especially in relation to* (nation branding) *campaigns.*

According to Moilanen, embassy level managers enjoy full autonomy and do not need to authorize online content before its publication. Thus, the ministry does not supervise embassy online activity but rather offers support, advice and training.

Information Dissemination

Authoring of online content at MFA level. Online content (i.e., SNS and websites) is authored by communications officers belonging to the communications department. Communications officers work in shifts in which they are responsible for following and commenting on world events and posting links to SNS content and websites. Communications officers enjoy autonomy and operate within ministry guidelines.

Issues to be addressed online by MFA. The Finnish MFA works in accordance with a yearly nation branding strategy and campaigns are translated into weekly themes. These themes include content, hashtags and multi-media. In addition, communications officers create content in accordance with ministry priorities and events taking place in real time (e.g., crisis communications). Other departments in the MFA do occasionally propose online content, yet this is translated into SNS content by communications officers. Such a routine is beneficial, as career diplomats identify issues that need to be addressed while communications officers ensure that such content is attractive to social media followers and is tailored to each platform (e.g., Twitter, YouTube).

Plurality of online channels. The majority of Finnish ministries do not coordinate online and SNS activity. However, the MFA does attempt to work closely with the prime minister's office, which is active on social media and deals with foreign policy issues. There are monthly meetings between the communications departments of most Finnish ministries, yet these deal with technical issues (e.g., creating a unified platform for all ministry websites) rather than coordination of messages. There are also weekly meetings between communications departments in several Finnish ministries, yet these focus on domestic rather than foreign media.

Nation branding activities are more closely synchronized, as the MFA coordinates the "This is Finland" campaign with all other stakeholders that have a vested interest in projecting a positive national image (e.g., ministries, financial corporations). Meetings are convened in order to ensure stakeholders author content relevant to weekly themes. This coordination may enable the MFA to project a coherent national image.

Authoring of online content at embassy level. The identity of digital diplomacy managers at the embassy varies greatly according to the size of Finnish missions. While the ambassador is responsible for all social media activity, online content in large embassies is authored by the assistant to the press officer, while in smaller embassies content is authored by the press officer or a local employee. Finnish press officers are not career diplomats but communications professionals recruited for these posts. In China and Japan, press officers are also fluent in the local language. This variation was evident in the study sample, as in London online content is authored by a 28-year-old local employee and a 42-year-old diplomat belonging to the Press and Culture Office, while content in Beijing and Tokyo is authored by Japanese and Chinese experts, ages 42 and 38 years old.

All embassy level managers emphasized the autonomy they enjoy in authoring SNS and website content. The Washington manager wrote:

> *The communications team creates content to the social media channels very independently. The press counselor is the supervisor of the team, and she reports to the ambassador. The communications team decides what topics to address in the social media. Sometimes we get input from the ministry, but most often we focus on local and timely themes . . .*

Issues to be addressed online by embassy. When asked what percentage of the embassy's online content originates from the ministry, four managers stated that 10% of the content is dictated by the ministry. Ministry-authored content seems to deal mainly with nation branding campaigns. The London manager wrote:

> *We decide tweets/posts at the embassy level following the social media, communications and country branding strategies of the embassy and MFA. We try and choose topics that are topical and relevant to the UK (or other English speaking audience). Sometimes we get recommendations from the MFA, for example regarding certain campaigns.*

The majority of respondents indicated that they regularly receive information and content from other departments in the embassy. Four of the five embassy managers stated that they participate in weekly meetings with other diplomats and are thus able to anticipate events and ask for relevant content. The Paris manager stated:

> *We have regular weekly meetings among the embassy's diplomats, which are led by our Ambassador. Our embassy is rather small and diplomats' offices are close to each other which means easy and quick sharing of information with all colleagues when necessary.*

When asked how they identify the MFA's priorities with regard to content, four of the five embassy managers stated that they follow the ministry's nation branding strategies. Managers also indicated that they routinely use the MFA-operated SNS accounts as a source of information regarding MFA priorities:

> *We follow the ministry's Twitter and Facebook accounts very closely to see what kind of content they are sharing.*

The exception to this rule was in the Chinese embassy, where tweets are authored by an external expert working with the ministry. Respondents' answers with regard to content and MFA priorities again suggest that the focus of the Finnish digital diplomacy model is nation branding.

Information Gathering

Information gathering at MFA level. The Finnish communications department does not follow foreign MFAs and embassies. In addition, the department rarely gathers information from social media and relays it to relevant departments.

This happens only when followers ask questions that the communications department cannot answer by itself. The department does, however, encourage diplomats to use social media as an information tool that is pertinent to their area of work. This modus operandi reflects a possible disadvantage, as the people most active on SNS do not use it as a source of information.

When asked if embassies provide the ministry with information gathered from social media, Moilanen answered that it is rare but might happen:

> *When the press officers might report on what happens in the local media they might include information on what is happening in the social media as well.*

Information gathering at embassy level. When asked how often they communicate with the ministry, and to what purpose, all managers stated that they communicate with the ministry on a weekly basis. However, such communication seems to be limited to receiving information and materials. The Paris manager wrote:

> *We communicate regularly. Communication might concern, for example, a media campaign or issue having large international media interest. A good example is the national PISA school performance results; we received tweet formulations and hashtags from Helsinki.*

The manager in Washington stated that:

> *We receive communications and country branding material and guidelines from the ministry on a regular basis.*

These answers suggest that embassies and the MFA exchange information on a regular basis while focusing on nation branding. No embassy managers stated that they collect information from SNS that may be of value to policy makers.

Public Diplomacy and Nation Branding

Nation branding at MFA level. Nation branding is the primary focus of the Finnish MFA's online activity. The "This is Finland" campaign includes Twitter channels and Facebook profiles targeted at anyone who is interested in Finland as well as websites that deal with tourism and investment opportunities. "This is Finland" includes SNS channels and websites in English, Chinese, Japanese,

Spanish, French, Portuguese and German. Such content is authored by the Public Diplomacy Unit.

Public diplomacy at MFA level. The Finnish MFA uses its Twitter account in order to communicate with, and *influence*, domestic and international media outlets and foreign policy experts. As Moilanen stated:

> *For foreign media it's important to explain the Finish stance on issues such as EU sanctions on Russia. If foreign media pick up on it, it's good, as it increases the reach of foreign policy messages to global audiences.*

Facebook is used to communicate with Finnish citizens and expats living abroad. Content on MFA operated Facebook profiles is published only in Finnish and Swedish and is meant to provide consular assistance and maintain ties with the Finnish diaspora.

The ministry routinely analyzes its audience base using analytic tools provided by SNS (e.g., Twitter analytics) while evaluating number of followers, type of followers and country of origin. According to Moilanen, nearly 80% of the ministry's SNS followers are Finish media outlets, Finnish foreign policy experts and Finns interested in politics. This is precisely the target audience defined by the MFA. It therefore appears that while nation branding activities are targeted at global audiences, foreign policy messages are targeted at Finnish citizens and newsroom elites. Notably, the Finnish MFA's digital diplomacy activities do not seem to target foreign populations.

Public engagement at MFA level. When asked to define engagement, a member of the communications department wrote:

> *Engagement in social media includes impressions, "Likes," shares, retweets, discussions, clicks on links… Yes, it is important. We are constantly thinking ways in which to increase engagement… make our content more interesting and engaging. We encourage communications officers and every MFA civil servant who is in social media to participate in relevant discussions.*

At the MFA level, engagement with followers focuses mainly on answering questions and correcting false information about Finland that may be circulating online. The ministry does not prohibit engagement with critics yet such engagement is limited to correcting false information while "*Spam content is usually best ignored.*" Moilanen stated that the MFA feels it's important to engage with followers "when this happens" suggesting audiences are not always in search of engagement.

Measuring public engagement at MFA level. The MFA is currently in the process of defining parameters for the evaluation of public diplomacy on SNS. This will include development of new analytical tools. Presently, the MFA uses figures such as number of followers, shares and clicks on links. According to Moilanen, these are "*superficial numbers*" as they say little about the quality of engagement with followers.

Public diplomacy and nation branding at embassy level. As is the case with the MFA, embassy digital diplomacy managers use Twitter in order to communicate with the local media, policy makers and the domestic population while Facebook is dedicated solely to communicating with the Finnish diaspora or people who have a special interest in Finland. This distinction suggests that the ministry has been able institute organizational working routines with each SNS. Facebook is also used to provide consular assistance to Finns. Interestingly, all embassy digital diplomacy managers listed the domestic population (e.g., Americans in the US) as the last group with which they aim to communicate. This could suggest that embassies prioritize communication with traditional elites over foreign populations. As the London manager wrote:

> *Twitter* (targets) *local press & media, think tanks, politicians, other decision makers, local population, Finnish people living in the UK. FB* (Facebook) *Local population* (*our audience base includes mainly Finnish people living in the UK*) *and British people with a connection to Finland.*

The Washington manager added:

> *On Twitter we try to reach local political and economic decision makers, think tanks, journalists, civic orgs and NGOs as well as the general public.*

The quote from the Washington manager seems to indicate that this embassy practices networked diplomacy, given a desire to communicate with non-state actors that influence foreign policy, such as think tanks and NGOs.

With regard to content at the embassy level, Twitter is used primarily for political messaging, nation branding and promotion of investment opportunities and Facebook is used for cultural issues and consular assistance to the Finnish diaspora.

Public engagement at embassy level. Moilanen stated that engaging with audiences is important, but he noted that embassy engagement may be limited due to lack of resources. Yet in their definitions of engagement, all embassy managers mentioned the issue of dialogue with SNS followers and their commitment to participating in online discussions. One social media manager stated that an ambassadors' SNS activity contributes to the embassy's ability to engage online, as they create a model to emulate.

> *If speaking about* (engagement in) *social media, it is a question of whether we are reactive or proactive in participating in relevant discussions, answering questions, addressing your messages to certain followers, etc.... Engagement largely depends on the working culture in the ministry or embassy in question. If one's supervisor is interested in social media... that might give you a guideline and a model as well.*

The manager from Beijing added that audiences are often called upon to engage with materials shared by the embassy, perhaps suggesting a form of collaboration.

> *During these campaigns* (promotional campaigns), *the followers are encouraged to comment on some special topic and they might also get incentives such as samples of products from Finnish companies.*

Many embassy managers referenced the need to correct misleading information about Finland. As this was one of the goals at the ministry level, it may be another example of this MFA's ability to meet organization-wide priorities. However, some embassy managers stated that while the MFA encourages engagement with followers, they do not feel that audiences are keen on engaging with the embassy, adding that engagement on the part of SNS followers is rare.

> *We are encouraged to engage... Large autonomy makes it easier... however we don't receive a great deal of them* (questions or comments). *On average we receive maybe 2–6 questions per week both on Twitter and on Facebook.*
>
> *Sometimes there are questions coming directly from followers, notably by journalists. Then of course we try to answer as soon as possible. That does not happen too often.*

When asked if the MFA prioritizes engagement with critics, embassy level managers stated that it's not a priority nor is it forbidden. When such engagement does occur, an emphasis is placed on correcting false information. The London manager wrote:

> *There's no priority but it's not forbidden either. We observe social media and debates & discussions... both positive and critical... If we notice clear misunderstandings... regarding the country, we'll try and correct them.*

Measuring public engagement at embassy level. An interesting finding was that the majority of managers tailored MFA content to their target audience with regard to local language (e.g., French) and culture thereby increasing the content's relevance. Likewise, Finnish embassies publish content in Finnish and Swedish targeting the Finnish diaspora. The Paris manager stated that:

> *Re-phrasing is needed mainly because of a different language. We also have to think about cultural context: posts that work in certain country do not necessarily function as well elsewhere... on our Facebook account we use the local language* (French) *and Finnish.*

However, in China and Japan, content is published solely in local languages. Not using English may be a disadvantage, as it limits the number of foreign embassies and global media outlets following Finnish missions to these countries.

Moilanen stated that from what he has observed, some embassies have been able to create communities of expats who use embassy social media accounts as an information guide.

> *Embassies have created communities, and it's usually the Finns that are there, it's more information for the people... In Thailand there has been unrest with people looking for information... turning to the Bangkok embassy Facebook page to know what the embassy is thinking about.*

All embassy managers stated that they analyze their audience on a regular basis with regard to occupation and country of origin. This enables Finnish embassies to analyze their ability to attract pre-defined audiences. Other parameters focus on reach of content (including number of followers, shares and re-tweets). Scope of dialogue is not measured.

Finally, embassy managers stated that they use feedback from followers in order to create more appealing content. This may be viewed as a tool for developing best practices at the embassy level. The Beijing manager wrote:

> *Surely, we notice what works and what doesn't. If some specific topic or way of doing things creates interest, certainly we want to invest more in it, and the other way around.*

Summary

The Finnish digital diplomacy model focuses mainly on nation branding activities that are coordinated by the MFA. Surprisingly, the MFA does not use social media for public diplomacy activities and online dialogue. Moreover, when the MFA does use social media for public diplomacy efforts, it focuses on informing and influencing elites, the Finnish population and the Finnish diaspora rather than foreign populations. Embassies are provided with branding materials, which they then disseminate online. Given the autonomy enjoyed by embassy level managers, the training of all diplomats and providing of online content, the Finnish digital diplomacy model may be characterized as "trust, train and provide." While the MFA coordinates nation branding activities with other stakeholders, no such effort is made to coordinate foreign policy messages. Such lack of coordination suggests an inability to overcome the challenge of plurality of online channels. In Finnish embassies, digital diplomacy seems to be an embassy-wide collaboration and managers are provided with materials by other departments. Both Finnish embassies and the MFA have yet to utilize SNS as an information source. While the MFA's online activities do not target foreign populations, embassy level managers did articulate the importance of engaging with foreign populations and collaborating with them online. However, engagement with critics is rare and limited to correcting false information.

Norway's MFA

Interview with Frode Overland, head of communication. Embassies that participated in the study: Jakarta, Abu Dhabi, Copenhagen, Madrid and Washington.

Structure of Digital Diplomacy Unit

The Norwegian MFA does not have a separate digital diplomacy unit and the press office is responsible for all communication, including online communication. Of the 15 employees comprising the press office, five are traditional spokespeople dealing with traditional media, five manage the MFA's websites and two are tasked with authoring social media content and supervising the digital diplomacy activities of the Norwegian mission. It is important to note that all members of the press office have access to SNS accounts and contribute content. The press office includes both trained diplomats and communications experts (i.e., former journalists). The press office, headed by Frode Overland, a former journalist and career diplomat, has only recently assumed all responsibility for the ministry's digital diplomacy activity. In the spring of

2015, all employees managing MFA web pages and social media platforms were transferred from the Section for Public Diplomacy and Web Information to the press office. This transition is demonstrative of the Norwegian MFA's belief that digital diplomacy should be used to augment the ministry's communication efforts. This was expressed by Overland, who said that digital diplomacy is a fully integrated and internalized approach to the MFA's communications work. According to Overland, having traditional and social media experts in the same unit creates an important synergy.

> *Sometimes they* (social media managers) *are very blunt with us and they say this tweet is boring… can't we rather focus on a different issue… because we see on Twitter that many people are tweeting about this issue but from a different angle.*

In this manner, press releases can address one dimension of an issue while online content would address another dimension.

The press office manages a social media empire consisting of more than 150 SNS accounts and a global network of websites operated at both the ministry and embassy level. Of the 15 employees, seven are under the age of 40 and the two employees who manage digital diplomacy efforts are digital natives under the age of 32.

Working Alongside Embassies

The Norwegian MFA offers a variety of digital diplomacy training courses with each course tailored to the needs of specific departments and positions. For instance, in the spring of 2015, the MFA conducted a seminar on the use of social media for press attachés. The ministry offers digital diplomacy training courses for all diplomats to be stationed abroad, consisting of a general introduction to social media, the manner in which SNS may be used to achieve diplomatic goals and practical skills necessary to use social media tools. New employees are introduced to MFA guidelines regarding the use SNS. Finally, the ministry offers one-on-one training for ambassadors.

The MFA's press office evaluates the websites and SNS profiles of all Norwegian embassies, especially those that have just recently migrated online or missions in which a new staff member has taken on the responsibility for digital diplomacy. Other activities include maintaining consistency across all websites and SNS profiles and ensuring that missions adhere to MFA guidelines. There is no direct supervision of content published by missions nor does the ministry tend to supply missions with social media content. As Overland stated:

> *I hope we will have more communication because it's been too compartmentalized so far. We* (press office) *have done our stuff here and they* (missions) *do their stuff abroad. We have not been able to harvest the full potential of doing social media campaigns all over the world.*

Information Dissemination

Authoring of online content at MFA level. Social media content published by the MFA is authored by press office staff members, be it traditional spokespersons who live-tweet from events, or staff members who manage websites and SNS profiles. The majority of the MFA's content is derived from the foreign minister's speeches, official state visits and press releases. Such content is published in both Norwegian and English, either by a designated staff member or the "on-duty" staff member during weekends and nights. Official state visits are intensely promoted online with hashtags, Twitter handles and tweets formulated in advance. Content authored by press office staffers is not approved before publication.

Issues to be addressed online by MFA. Most of the content published by the MFA is based on source material provided by other departments. Digital diplomacy is thus an MFA-wide collaboration in which departments identify foreign policy issues to be addressed while the press office translates these issues into SNS content. The MFA also collaborates on the promotion of major political events (e.g., United Nations General Assembly). In such cases, the press office receives materials from relevant departments and offers online coverage of the event. Press packages may also be sent to the embassies, but there is no requirement to use this information.

Plurality of online channels. According to Overland, there is no formal channel of communication between the MFA and other ministries that are also active online. However, there is an effort to coordinate messages with spokespersons of other ministries on issues of common concern (e.g., troop deployments to Iraq). Overland stated that the MFA does not feel that plurality of channels is a major challenge, as:

> *We know very well what our responsibility is as the MFA and where that responsibility ends and becomes the responsibility of the MOD (Ministry of Defense).*

Authoring of online content at embassy level. The identity of the embassy digital diplomacy managers varies with the size of Norwegian embassies. In larger embassies, the press or cultural attachés will be responsible for digital diplomacy while in smaller embassies it is the domain of a local employee who is a skilled communications expert. Due to a lack of resources, only the largest Norwegian embassies have a dedicated staffer responsible solely for digital diplomacy. Thus, embassy mangers are usually a "jack of all trades." This variety was evident in the study sample. In Copenhagen, online content is authored by a 37-year-old local employee, in Washington it is authored by a 45-year-old employee while in Abu Dhabi the author is a 62-year-old ambassador. Interestingly, several digital diplomacy managers stated that they report to the Ambassador who is "the head editor." This may be the reason why the MFA offers intensive social media training to Ambassadors.

All embassy managers expressed their autonomy with regard to content published online stating that they do not confer with the MFA before publishing content. The Madrid manager wrote:

> *I decide depending on the embassy's communication strategy, depending on the target group and highlighting the topics on our communication plan...*
>
> *I can decide the topic on our social media accordingly... I have autonomy with regard to which tweets or posts to publish. I do not need authorization from my supervisor for each post and tweet.*

In other embassies, managers may need to confer with the ambassador, as the Twitter channel is in his name.

Issues to be addressed online by embassy. Four of the five embassy managers stated that between 1% and 5% of all content published online is provided by the MFA. The 62-year-old ambassador, on the other hand, stated that nearly 50% of the content published online by his embassy is derived from the ministry. This may represent a generational gap in which digital natives find it easier to author online content. However, it may also be a result of the fact that the ambassador himself publishes content alongside many other responsibilities. A press office staffer stated:

> *I will share social media content* (with Norwegian missions) *when appropriate and possible. Embassies are also encouraged to reuse material we post on the MFA's accounts.*

All embassy managers stated that they routinely receive content from their colleagues and that creation of online content is an embassy-wide collaboration. Most embassy managers partake in weekly meetings in which topics and events are discussed. In Madrid, each embassy employee is responsible for providing online content relating to his field (e.g., culture, consular). In

Washington, the embassy is divided into teams working on specific issues (e.g., the Arctic) and each team has a representative from the communications department. As the Washington manager wrote:

> *I am part of the Arctic team and work on many cultural projects, so I focus my digital diplomacy on Arctic messaging.*

The embassy-wide collaboration on online content creation is a unique feature of Norwegian digital diplomacy.

When answering the question, "How do you know what topics are regarded as a priority by the ministry?" there seems to be another generational gap. Digital natives seem to be more prone towards using the MFA's SNS accounts in order to learn its priorities, while the older managers in Washington (age 45) and Abu Dhabi (age 62) rely mostly on official communication from the ministry.

Information Gathering

Information gathering at MFA level. The MFA encourages diplomats to use Twitter as an information source in order to get acquainted with a country to which they are about to be posted or gain insight into specific issues (e.g., the Arctic). According to Overland, diplomats are encouraged to use Twitter for information gathering even if they do not wish to be active on it. Thus, some diplomats may be lurkers using SNS for information gathering rather than active participation. Overland stated that

> *With a 20-second search on Twitter you will probably be better orientated than spending an hour scrolling through various ministries' websites.*

The MFA also gathers information from social media. According to Overland, the press office routinely shares such information with relevant ministerial departments. In addition, some embassies include information from social media when reporting to the MFA. However, such reports occur mainly during times of crisis when embassies follow guidelines that place an emphasis on information gathering from local SNS.

> *The area where we have come the furthest is crisis management where we have a set of guidelines for how to use social media ... For instance now in Nepal, they* (the embassy) *are following the crisis manual where we have a different set of rules for social media ... Now we need to take it a step further for day to day work.*

Information gathering at embassy level. Despite the MFA's emphasis on gathering information from SNS, embassies have yet to adopt this practice. Moreover, communication between embassy managers and the MFA appears to be sporadic and issue-based. One embassy manager stated that he communicates with the MFA *"Not on a regular basis. I communicate with the ministry for advice."* The only embassy level manager to mention the use of social media for information gathering stated that:

> *There is some form of communication at least monthly. Usually email exchanges of information. Often reporting.*

Public Diplomacy and Nation Branding

Nation branding at MFA level. Currently, the MFA does not manage nation branding campaigns; these are under the supervision of tourism authorities, while the "Innovation Norway" campaign is managed by the Ministry of Trade, Industry and Fisheries and local authorities. This separation between nation branding and public diplomacy activities, as well as the multitude of actors involved in nation branding activities, seem to demonstrate the challenge of plurality of channels. Since Overland stated that there are no official channels of coordination, one has to wonder if this does not limit the MFA's ability to author a coherent and consistent national narrative.

Public diplomacy at MFA level. The Norwegian MFA operates two Twitter channels (English, Norwegian), and two Facebook profiles (English, Norwegian). One Facebook profile is used for news dissemination while the other focuses on consular information. In addition, the MFA manages the ministry's section on the government's website (www.regjeringen.no) alongside its own websites in English and Norwegian (www.mfa.no) and a travel advice website (www.landsider.no). All these online channels deal mainly with foreign policy issues.

The Norwegian MFA uses Facebook and Twitter in order to reach different audiences. Facebook content targets the domestic Norwegian population and offers information in the form of narrative storytelling. According to Overland, people on Facebook are usually not interested in political messaging but prefer stories that communicate policy initiatives. Thus, Facebook content is used to demonstrate the MFA's activities and how these serve Norway.

> *For instance, a development aid project in Africa where you educate girls. You would have a lot of pictures and videos on female empowerment. But you would not start hardcore political messaging on Facebook.*

Twitter, on the other hand, is used for what Overland calls "elite political communication" which targets the media, foreign policy experts, other MFAs and NGOs. Given his assertion that Facebook is for local consumption, and Twitter for communication with elites, the Norwegian MFA does not seem to place an emphasis on reaching foreign populations through SNS. A staffer who did mention the general public in her answer, seen below, listed it as the last group the MFA targets.

> *Target audience varies from account to account and platform to platform, but includes journalists/media outlets, other MFAs, ministers and senior officials, academia, NGOs... and the general public.*

This statement may be demonstrative of a network mentality in which MFAs target non-state actors such as NGOs, academic institutions and international organizations.

Public engagement at MFA level. When asked to define the term "engagement," a press office staffer wrote that:

> *Engagement to me is based on the requirement in the Norwegian Constitution which states that "The authorities of the state shall create conditions that facilitate open and enlightened public discourse." This includes providing information on the ministry and minister's activities... and allowing for comments, questions and responses from the public.*

While this definition seems to include both foundations of the relational approach to diplomacy (i.e., engagement and listening) it also seems to focus on the need to communicate with the Norwegian population rather than foreign populations.

In his interview, Overland stated that the MFA does not feel its followers are keen on engaging with it.

> *The thing is that we are not very often challenged on Twitter or social media at all... I'm surprised how little challenged we are... how few questions we are getting. We are getting a few questions on Facebook but that's consular issues... on Twitter, normally when we are challenged it's by NGOs and pressure groups that challenges us on a certain issue and it doesn't demand a reply as such, other than stating our policy.*

It is possible that the lack of engagement observed by Overland is a result of the fact that the MFA does not actively target foreign populations. Moreover, when asked if the MFA places an emphasis on engagement, a staffer stated that:

> *We respond to general queries when possible and appropriate. However, most of the messages directed to us are not questions as such, but more expressions of opinions… We do not usually respond to these.*

The policy of not responding to opinions expressed by followers may also contribute to the MFAs feeling that it is not being engaged with.

Finally, when asked if the MFA engages with critics, press office staffers answered that they routinely correct false information but do not:

> *Get involved in protracted discussions on social media with critics or one-cause activists (e.g., Norway's position on whaling, the Middle East).*

Measuring public engagement at MFA level. The main parameter used by the MFA to evaluate its public diplomacy activity is whether SNS channels attract pre-defined target audiences. Thus, the quality of followers outweighs the number of followers. Other parameters focus on reach of content in terms of number of re-tweets, "Likes" and shares. Notably, none of these parameters evaluate scope of dialogue.

Public diplomacy at embassy level. Like the MFA, the majority of Norwegian embassies in the sample use Facebook in order to reach the Norwegian diaspora and the local population while Twitter is used for the local press, policy makers, influencers and the local population. As is the case with the MFA, Facebook is used more for cultural affairs, investment promotion and consular activity, while Twitter is used for political messaging. As the Washington manager wrote:

> *On Facebook we focus on the general US public with an interest in Norway, especially the Norwegian-American population. The content is concentrated more on culture, less on policy… We use Twitter for more focused policy outreach… and much more policy centered messaging, aiming for press, think-tanks and professionals.*

Yet the languages used by Norwegian embassies may inhibit their ability to reach their target audiences. For instance, the embassy in Copenhagen publishes content solely in Norwegian. Lack of content in English may prevent the diplomatic milieu and international new outlets from following this embassy.

Similarly, the embassy in Spain only uses Spanish thus preventing Norwegians and Norwegian news outlets from following their missions abroad.

Public engagement at embassy level. When asked to define "engagement," four of the five embassy managers replied that engagement improves Norway's digital presence and promotes Norway's interests. Only one manager referenced the need to foster dialogue with online publics stating that engagement was "*Interacting with everyone, from all levels, and not just a selected few.*" The manager from Washington did not reference dialogue but did mention the embassy's use of Skype in order to facilitate conversations between the ambassador and US university students. When asked if engagement with followers was emphasized by the MFA, and how often they actually engage with followers, the ambassador in Abu Dhabi stated that while "*actual engagement is quite rare,*" all questions posed by followers are answered. Another embassy manager stated:

> (MFA emphasis on engagement) *Not so much. Content and reaching the right audience is more important*... (actual engagement) *not too often. Every 2 weeks on average.*

With regard to engaging with critics, an interesting difference arose between the local employees and the Ambassador. The majority of embassy managers stated that while engaging with critics is not forbidden, they tend to not get involved in such debates except when correcting information posted by followers. One embassy manager wrote:

> *From time to time there are campaigns directed towards Norway or Norwegian interests, and we deal with them on a case to case basis.*

This answer is in line with comments made by other managers according to which they communicate with the MFA "*when a campaign is waged against Norway's policies*". These, along with statements made by Overland, may reflect a tendency to view NGOs as being extremely critical of Norway, which may reduce willingness to engage with them out of fear of losing control over the communication process. Interestingly, the ambassador in Abu Dhabi stated adamantly that engaging with critics is a priority. This may reflect a generational gap between younger diplomats and the ambassador, who has developed the skills and confidence necessary to engage with critics, and views it as an opportunity rather than a risk.

Measuring public engagement at embassy level. When asked how often they analyze their target audience, only two managers stated that they do so on a regular basis (e.g., once a month). Other answers included "once per year," "seldom" and "from time to time." When asked about parameters they used for evaluating online activity, most answers focused on general statistics such as re-tweets, shares and "Likes."

With regard to tailoring MFA content to the local context, three managers stated that they simply re-tweet MFA content. One manager wrote that:

> *We re-tweet if we find them interesting in our local context. If not, we try to find a local angel before posting.*

There was a visible generational gap between the digital natives and immigrants in developing digital diplomacy best practices. All three managers aged below 40 stated that they use feedback from SNS content in order to improve future posts. The immigrants, like the 45-year-old manger in Washington, stated:

> *Only if we realize we have made mistakes. The speed and frequency of daily communication across several digital platforms makes mistakes inevitable.*

Summary

Norway's digital diplomacy rests on training all diplomats, especially high-ranking ones, in the art of digital diplomacy. The focus on training digital immigrants represents an attempt to fully reap the benefits of social media use. The creation of online content appears to be an organization-wide collaboration at both the ministry and embassy level. Surprisingly, the MFA does not supervise embassy online activity or provide embassies with content. The Norwegian digital diplomacy model may thus be characterized as "train, collaborate and trust." Generational gaps between digital natives and immigrants were observed in both content creation and working routines at the embassy level. However, an opposite generational gap was observed, as the most experienced diplomat—in contrast to younger digital diplomacy managers—stressed the importance of engaging with critics. While SNS are used as an information source at the MFA level, embassies have yet to embrace this working routine, suggesting a lack of ability to implement organization-wide working routines. Plurality of channels is not regarded by the MFA as a major challenge despite the fact that nation branding activities are all conducted by other governmental agencies. While the MFA expressed a feeling that SNS followers aren't keen on engaging in dialogue, this may be a result of the ministry and embassies' unwillingness to engage with critics of Norway or SNS followers expressing opinions.

Israel's MFA

Interview with Yoram Morad, director of Digital Diplomacy Unit. Embassies that participated in the study: Washington, Santiago, Berlin, London and Buenos Aries.

Structure of Digital Diplomacy Unit

The Israeli Digital Diplomacy Department belongs to the media and public affairs division, which is part of the Public Diplomacy Directorate. The Digital Diplomacy Department is made up of four branches: the internet branch, which is responsible for the MFA's main English website and provides support for embassy webmasters; the new media branch, which is responsible for MFA SNS profiles and training; a language-based branch that is responsible for online content in Arabic, Russian, Persian and Hebrew; and a fourth branch that deals with innovation in the digital space. The MFA is active on Facebook, Twitter, Google +, Instagram, Flickr, Pinterest, YouTube and Weibo. In total, the MFA manages more than 250 SNS profiles.

The Department is composted of 12 employees, the majority of whom are communications and social media experts. The unit is headed by Yoram Morad, a trained diplomat. While the age of department staffers ranges from 19 to 60, most MFA level digital diplomacy managers are between the ages of 30 and 40.

Working Alongside Embassies

The Digital Diplomacy Department is in charge of training diplomats, providing assistance to Israeli missions and supervising their online activity. The department offers two forms of training. The first is a course that introduces new employees and diplomats stationed abroad to the MFA's digital diplomacy activity. Such courses offer practical training, development of skills and an overview of how online communication has impacted the practice of diplomacy. Secondly, the MFA convenes annual seminars intended for embassy level digital diplomacy managers.

> *Such training is week-long, and is aimed at thoroughly going through the main social media platform and best practices in each of them.*

Embassy level managers do not require MFA authorization before publishing online content. However, missions' channels are frequently visited by the Digital Diplomacy Department in order to ensure relevance and accuracy of content and proper use of the medium (e.g., Twitter). The scope of communication between the MFA and its missions abroad varies greatly. As an MFA staffer wrote:

It depends on the mission—with some there's an almost daily contact, with others it's less frequent and could be weeks.

Finally, missions and diplomats are continuously encouraged to engage with online followers and, more specifically, with online critics. An MFA staffer wrote:

Answering criticism is another opportunity to present Israel's case and it also shows respect and open mindedness.

Many times, the MFA utilizes missions abroad in order to increase the reach of online content. As Morad explains, by disseminating information on both MFA and mission SNS accounts the number of people exposed to content increases dramatically as does the variety of the audience. This enables the MFA to reach diverse spheres of influence.

We begin by spearing these messages through the people in our department. Then we recruit our diplomats stationed abroad and our embassies. Then, these messages find their way to our embassies' followers, who distribute the messages to their own online communities.

Cooperation between the ministry and missions abroad is often achieved through dedicated regional Facebook groups (e.g., North America) which are composed of MFA staffers and embassy level digital diplomacy managers.

Information Dissemination

Authoring of online content at MFA level. The majority of online content published by the MFA is authored by the Digital Diplomacy Department. Interestingly, the MFA often publishes the same content on numerous SNS. As a department staffer explained

Because our goal is to get our message across to the largest audience possible, we will disseminate that message through all our channels ... while making necessary adaptations for each and every platform.

Another staffer stated that lack of resources often precludes the MFA from creating different content for each SNS.

Members of the Digital Diplomacy Department enjoy full autonomy when publishing content and do not require authorization from superiors. MFA content deals mainly with foreign policy issues and nation branding activities.

According to an MFA staffer, message dissemination remains the focus of the MFA's online activity.

> *The message hasn't changed. We have a new medium for delivering the message, but it's the message that still counts. The medium influences how you get the message across.*

The MFA's English language Facebook page serves as an information center for missions abroad and includes foreign policy issues as well as nation branding materials. On Twitter, the MFA operates two separate accounts, one dedicated to policy news and another dedicated to nation branding.

Issues to be addressed online by MFA. While the Digital Diplomacy Department is in charge of formulating online content, the issues to be addressed online are decided upon by additional departments in the Public Diplomacy Directorate. Likewise, content may originate from other MFA departments, yet not on a regular basis.

> *There is a separate department in the ministry that is in charge of phrasing and deciding what content will be disseminated. Our department deals mainly with dissemination of information and engagement. Our expertise lies in taking foreign policy messages ... and spreading them virally.*

This model offers important benefits, as trained diplomats recognize events and issues that must be addressed while the translation of these messages into appealing online content is in the hands of social media experts.

Plurality of online channels. Within the MFA, the challenge of plurality of channels has yet to be fully addressed. This is due to the fact that there are several SNS profiles that are operated by the other departments in the ministry. For instance, the MFA's Cultural Department manages a Facebook profile dedicated to promoting Israeli culture (CultureBuzz Israel) while the international organizations division manages a green technology and environment Facebook profile (Green Israel). MFA staffers did not illustrate how inter-organizational coordination is achieved, stating only that other departments are consulted with "*when the need arises*." The fact that other departments publish online content that shapes Israel's image may inhibit the Digital Diplomacy Department's ability to narrate a coherent and consistent Israeli narrative.

When asked if they coordinate content with other governmental ministries also active online, MFA staffers answered that a forum of new media managers in Israeli ministries convenes every few months in order to present their online activity and share best practices. Government-wide coordination is most evident during times of crisis (e.g., military operations, Nepal earthquake). The issue of plurality of channels is especially relevant to Israel given the number of ministries involved in Israeli foreign policy. This was most evident in the previous government as the communication minister was in charge of Israeli-U.S. relations, Israel's justice minister was in charge of negotiations with the Palestinians, and Israel's economy minister was in charge of relations with the global Jewish diaspora.

Authoring of online content at embassy level. In all Israeli embassies participating in this study online content was authored by local employees who belong to the public diplomacy department. The ages of the digital diplomacy managers varied greatly. In Washington, the manager is a 30-year-old employee, while in Santiago the author is 47 years old. Three of the five managers participating in this sample were digital natives.

All managers expressed their autonomy with regard to authoring and publishing online content. However, all five also stated that they use this autonomy when dealing with "soft" issues. Political issues, or those deemed as sensitive by the embassy manager, are usually approved by a superior. Such working routines may suggest that local employees realize their limited ability to author content dealing with complex foreign policy issues and thus seek guidance from trained diplomats.

Issues to be addressed online by embassy. When asked what percentage of online content published by the embassy is derived from the MFA, a generational gap was observed. Digital natives stated that the MFA provides between 5–8% of online content, while digital immigrants stated that between 50–65% of online content is provided by the MFA. As one digital native wrote:

> *Topics are drawn from multiple sources including centrally from the MFA … Topics are also based on trending news and media, interesting or exciting endeavors coming out of Israel, and local activities of the embassy.*

When asked how they identify MFA priorities, the majority of managers stated that they rely on communication with the MFA (e.g., email) or interaction with other diplomats. Only one embassy manager stated that "*We constantly check their* (MFA) *website and Facebook page.*" This finding is surprising, given the fact that the MFA views its own SNS profiles as an information center meant to serve embassy managers. This gap could suggest a lack of ability to implement MFA-wide working routines.

While embassy managers enjoy autonomy, they are at times instructed by the MFA to publish content as part of a global campaign. According to an MFA staffer, issues of global importance range from nation branding and promotional videos, to the struggle against terror and Israeli aid following natural disasters (e.g., Nepal earthquake).

When asked if they receive information from other departments in the embassy, mangers' answers ranged from "*rarely*" to "*frequently*" and "*not as often as we should.*" The majority of managers stated that they do not receive information from other departments, with one manager adding:

> *We receive information from other employees, but not as often as we should; maybe once every 2–3 weeks. Our channels should better showcase the activities of the mission.*

In addition, only one manager stated that he routinely attends embassy meetings in which he may gather information and prepare content for upcoming events.

Information Gathering

Information gathering at MFA level. When asked if they use SNS as an information source, MFA staffers stated that gathering information from SNS is now an established working routine. One staffer wrote:

> *I do browse through some social media accounts of foreign ministries, embassies and diplomats... like many tweeters, I also use Twitter as a source of information to learn about political and diplomatic issues.*

However, the Digital Diplomacy Department does not regularly disseminate information gathered online to relevant desks and departments within the MFA. Likewise, embassy managers are not required to collect such information for the ministry.

Information gathering at embassy level. When asked how often and to what end they communicate with the MFA, embassy managers stated that they regularly communicate with the ministry in order to seek advice, receive technical support and gather feedback on their activity. No embassy managers stated that they relay information from local social media platforms to the MFA.

Public Diplomacy and Nation Branding Activity

Between nation branding and public diplomacy. On Twitter, the MFA distinguishes between public diplomacy and nation branding activities. The @Israel account is used to brand Israel, while the @IsraelMFA account is used for public diplomacy activities including engagement with online publics. The MFA's English Facebook profile, on the other hand, deals with issues relating to Israeli foreign relations and Israeli national achievements (e.g., culture, science).

Nation branding at MFA level. The @Israel Twitter channel is used solely for branding the state of Israel. As such, content featured on this channel deals with Israeli cultural achievements, lifestyle, promotion of tourism and Israeli technological innovation. The subject of Israeli innovation was repeatedly mentioned by MFA staffers, probably due to the fact that Israel's branding campaigns focus on portraying it as a technological pioneer and a "start-up nation." As an MFA staffer wrote:

> *Science and technology is where we find Israel's relative advantage.*

Nation-branding content is also published on the MFA's English language Facebook profile. In addition, the MFA operates SNS channels dedicated to specific aspects of Israel's image. These include the "Culturebuzz Israel" Facebook profile dedicated to promoting Israeli culture; a green technology Facebook profile (Green Israel) and the @IsraelEconomy Twitter channel which is managed by the Economic Division and deals with investment opportunities. MFA websites deal with two main issues: the "Israel Experience," which focuses on lifestyle and cultural achievement, and "Innovative Israel," which focuses on scientific and technological achievements.

Public diplomacy at MFA level. The Israeli MFA uses its English language Facebook and Twitter channels in order to communicate with foreign populations and news outlets. The MFA also operates several SNS profiles in foreign languages, which are used to reach specific foreign populations and media organizations. These include channels in Arabic, Russian, Persian and Hebrew. Morad stated that a byproduct of digital diplomacy activity is a more structured approach to public diplomacy, as one can define a specific target audience he wishes to reach and evaluate whether this audience has in fact been reached.

> *In our case, we operate under the assumption that 25% of people will never be receptive to our messages. There is also another 25% percent who needs no convincing... So we decided not to bother with these audiences and focus on the 50% in the middle, those who might be receptive to our messages.*

In their answers, MFA staffers placed a great emphasis on Arab social media users willing to engage with Israel. While journalists and policy makers were also mentioned, the Arab audience was more visible among all members of the Digital Diplomacy Department. This was best demonstrated by a staffer who discussed the ability to bypass traditional gatekeepers:

> *Think about how dependent we once were on traditional gatekeepers such as newspaper editors in terms of getting our message across. Nowadays, we are much less dependent on them. For instance you can have a very successful viral campaign without going through those gatekeepers.*

Public engagement at MFA level. When asked to define "engagement," one MFA staffer stated that it was the need to "*Keep the conversation going, where it's possible.*" Another staffer defined it as "*Communicating with the audience in every way possible and through various channels.*" Both these definitions suggest a conceptual approach that values dialogue rather than message dissemination. Indeed, the Israeli MFA seems to place an emphasis on engagement; and missions are directly instructed to engage in dialogue with their audiences. One MFA staffer wrote:

> *Our Facebook page in the Arabic language is one of the most engaging social media accounts we have... There is a lot of dialogue taking place there between the ministry and its followers... most of the people who arrive at this Facebook page have never spoken to Israelis... now, they have a unique opportunity to speak to us... and to hear our side of the story.*

When asked if the ministry places an emphasis on engaging with critics, a staffer wrote that this was one of the MFA's main activities. Another staffer added:

> *When we began using social media our unit placed an emphasis on providing responses to such criticism... over the years, we have developed a vibrant online community... its members increasingly respond to criticism themselves.*

In an attempt to illustrate the MFA's model of engagement, Morad and other staffers focused yet again on Arab SNS users, stating that:

> *One objective we set was to promote our Facebook profile in Arabic. We know we were successful... because we doubled the number of "Likes"... In addition, the number of comments was five times higher than before.*

Measuring pubic engagement at MFA level. The previous comment by Morad suggests that the MFA evaluates digital diplomacy activities in terms of dialogue, such as number of comments, in addition to reach of content. When asked what parameters are used to measure public engagement, staffers mentioned "Likes," shares, numbers of comments and the "talking about this" parameters that "*also tell you something about your reach. The more people talk about you, the greater your potential reach.*" These answers are somewhat contradictory to Morad's statement, as they mostly deal with reach of content rather than scope of dialogue.

Public diplomacy and nation branding at the embassy level. Digital diplomacy managers at the embassy level are in charge of both public diplomacy and nation branding activities. When asked who their target audience was, the majority of authors stated they target the local population, influencers and opinion leaders. The Berlin manager stated:

> *Through Facebook we mainly try to attract the local population and through Twitter the population and also the local press.*

With regard to languages, embassy managers stated that they only use the local language (e.g., Spanish in Argentina). Such use of languages may inhibit the embassy's ability to practice networked diplomacy, as they do not use English for the diplomatic milieu or Hebrew for consular affairs and the Israeli diaspora abroad.

Public engagement at embassy level. When asked to define the term "engagement," each embassy manager offered a different definition, suggesting that the MFA has yet to adopt an organization-wide definition. The manager in Santiago stated that engagement was "*Finding the 'common base' between our strengths and the public interest*" while the manger in Berlin stated that engagement is "(audiences) *giving us feedback and writing comments.*" There was, however, a generational gap, as all three digital natives mentioned the issue of dialogue—in contrast to immigrants, who spoke of common interests or were unable to offer a definition of the term.

Four of the five embassy managers stated that they engage with followers on a weekly or daily basis. However, when asked who their target audience was, only two of the five embassy managers specifically identified the local population as a target audience in addition to the local press, policy makers and opinion makers. Moreover, only one embassy manager identified the local Jewish diaspora as an important target audience. This seems to be at odds with the MFA's emphasis on dialogue. Moreover, some managers stated that they answer only certain kinds of questions:

> *We answer all serious inquiries delivered to us via private messages or as comments on our posts. We do not, however, answer general questions that come up in discussions, such as why did Israel react in such a way?*

With regard to engaging with critics, three of the five embassy managers stated that it was not a priority for the MFA, a statement that is in contradiction to that made by MFA staffers. The prevailing sentiment expressed by embassy managers was that they are willing to engage with critics who are open to dialogue, a comment in line with Morad's strategy of engaging with the 50% who are open to Israeli messaging.

> *We do put some emphasis on engaging with people who criticize but we will only engage with those that we see as rational and have the potential to shift their opinion. We will not engage with those who clearly have no interest in hearing our side of the story.*

Measuring public diplomacy at embassy level. When asked how often they analyze their target audience, answers ranged from "weekly" and "all the time" to "only during crises," suggesting a lack of MFA-wide working routines. Parameters used by embassy managers to evaluate online activity included reach (e.g., re-tweets, number of followers) in addition to dialogic parameters (e.g., number of replies, number of comments) suggesting an organizational view that values the quality of followers and not just the number of followers.

Four of the five embassy managers stated that they re-phrase and tailor MFA online content to the local population in terms of culture, interests and language. As one manager wrote:

> *Sometimes I have to rephrase them because they are not [adapted to the] Argentinian mentality and they are in Hebrew or in English.*

Finally, the digital natives stated that they use feedback to identify their followers' areas of interest. The digital immigrants, on the other hand, stated that they use feedback to identify mistakes and content that should have not been published.

Summary

The Israeli MFA often utilizes its missions abroad in order to expand the reach of its online content and its ability to target diverse online networks and audiences. For this reason, the MFA may post the same content on different SNS, a finding that was not hypothesized in the research questions. Given its emphasis on training both MFA and embassy level staff, and its supervision of content published by missions abroad, the Israeli digital diplomacy model is one of "train, supervise and utilize." While the issues to be addressed online are decided upon by other MFA departments, the Digital Diplomacy Department's expertise lies in translating foreign policy messages into attractive and engaging content. Surprisingly, despite the fact that other departments, not to mention numerous other ministries, also publish online content, the MFA does not routinely coordinate content with other stakeholders. While the MFA's SNS accounts are meant to serve as an information guide for embassies, these mostly rely on official communication with the MFA. In contrast to previous studies, this analysis finds that using SNS as an information source has yet to become a routine practice by Israeli embassies. While the MFA seems to place a focus on fostering dialogue with foreign populations, namely Arab SNS users, embassy level managers' responses indicate that they only engage with followers on specific issues and are reluctant to engage with critics of Israel. Embassy level managers do seem to place a focus on tailoring online content to their local audiences.

Discussion

The term "digital disruption" relates to the positive and negative outcomes digitalization has had on private and public institutions (Deloitte, 2012; Hocking & Melissen, 2015). Indeed, such outcomes are often result of necessity not choice. As organizations, news outlets and individuals began to migrate online, governments were soon to follow. For foreign ministries, digitalization has brought opportunities and threats. On the one hand, MFAs have found a new means with which to achieve diplomatic goals, such as aiding citizens in times of crisis, communicating with foreign populations, strengthening their national brand and re-connecting with their diasporas.

On the other hand, MFAs now encounter challenges from within government as well as outside of it. From within government, MFAs may have lost their position as coherent narrators of their national image and policies, given the migration of numerous governmental bodies to social media. MFAs now also operate in contested online arenas in which citizen journalists, media outlets and foreign governments all frame government action and compete over audience attention (Hayden, 2012). Likewise, MFAs and diplomats must now contend with a knowledgeable, empowered and unpredictable population, who may support or criticize governments online. As Alec Ross, Senior Advisor for Innovation to Secretary of State Hillary Clinton, said, "The 21st century is a really terrible time to be a control freak" (Lichtenstein, 2010). Lastly, the rules of diplomatic engagement have changed in recent years, as diplomats and MFAs are now expected to continually share information and speak with, rather than at, online publics.

Digital diplomacy studies have only recently begun to investigate the strategies MFAs employ to overcome the challenges and reap the benefits of SNS (Kampf, Manor & Segev, 2015). While these studies have shed light on the emerging practice of digital diplomacy, most have not adopted an integrated viewpoint that analyzes digital diplomacy at three important levels: the embassy, the ministry and government as a whole. Moreover, studies have failed to analyze the manner in which MFAs themselves conceptualize digital diplomacy and articulate its goals. Do MFAs place a premium on online engagement? Do they view social media as an important component of 21st century diplomacy? And do they view it is a mass media tool or social media tool?

Digitalization has necessitated that MFAs adapt to a new technological and social landscape. This has brought about a need to institutionalize digital diplomacy through the formulation of guidelines and best practices, the training of diplomats and the creation of departments tasked with its practice. This aspect of digital diplomacy has been neglected by contemporary studies, as has an evaluation of the identity of digital diplomacy practitioners.

This study attempted to address these gaps by thoroughly analyzing the digital diplomacy models adopted by four mid-sized MFAs. Moreover, it aimed to do so through the prism of a constitutive approach to IR (Wendt, 1998) by understanding how the practitioners of digital diplomacy constitute and conceptualize this form of diplomacy. By interviewing practitioners of digital diplomacy at the MFA level and collecting information from embassy level practitioners through questionnaires, this study aimed to answer the question, "Have MFAs realized the potential of digital diplomacy?" Yet this question was but a stepping stone towards a greater goal—understanding how MFAs vary in their use of social media and what explains this variance.

This study's first research question focused on the manner which MFAs have integrated social media into their working routines. Results indicate that online content at the MFA level is authored solely by communication or social media experts (e.g., former journalists, spokespersons) rather than trained diplomats. However, while these experts author content, they do not necessarily decide what issues shall be addressed online. In the Finnish model, content is derived from a yearly branding strategy, while in the Israeli and Norwegian models, career diplomats identify issues to be addressed online, which are then translated into online content by social media experts. The incorporation of career diplomats in MFA models seems to counterbalance the predominance of communication experts in the practice of digital diplomacy. This is an important finding, for while communication experts are able to author viral content, they may lack the skills necessary to identify issues and events that must be addressed by the MFA and to deconstruct complex foreign policy issues. It is the collaboration between career diplomats and communications experts that best characterizes the four digital diplomacy models identified in this study.

Across all MFAs sampled, the majority of embassy level digital diplomacy managers were local employees as opposed to career diplomats. This was even the case in larger embassies such as the Norwegian, Finnish and Israeli embassies to Washington D.C. Most interviewees stated that local employees may be tasked with digital diplomacy activity out of a lack of resources, a finding that questions the cost effectiveness of digital diplomacy. The predominance of local employees at the embassy level presents MFAs with both challenges and benefits. Local employees may increase the relevance of SNS content by tailoring it to the characteristics of domestic audiences (e.g., language, culture, history). However, such employees may lack the skills necessary to explain complex foreign policy issues and respond to criticism by online followers.

Another consistent finding is MFAs' encouragement of career diplomats to migrate online while aiding them in developing the skills necessary to do so. Across all MFAs sampled, diplomats slated to be stationed abroad and digital diplomacy managers at the embassy level partake in compulsory social media training courses, which introduce MFA guidelines for using online platforms and offer practical skills such as operating SNS profiles, creating attractive online content and conveying foreign policy issues in narrative form for a blog. Such training may be viewed as a tool for institutionalizing digital diplomacy as organization-wide working routines are developed alongside best practices (Vance, 2012; McNutt, 2014). Institutional-wide working routines were identified in all four MFAs with regard to use of SNS to reach specific target audiences, public engagement with online followers, interaction with online critics and use of SNS in times of crisis (e.g., Nepal earthquake).

Certain MFAs seem to place particular emphasis on training ambassadors in the use of SNS. In the Polish MFA, the spokesman annually addresses a forum of all ambassadors gathered in Warsaw, while the Norwegian MFA offers ambassadors one-on-one training sessions. Such training is imperative, as ambassadors are responsible for online content published by their embassies. Should ambassadors fail to realize the significance of using online tools, or treat SNS with suspicion, their embassy's online activity may be non-existent. This study therefore finds that ambassadors are new gatekeepers in the digital world and as such they require a new set of skills.

The overall encouragement of diplomats to migrate online may represent a shift in MFA mentality, which Copeland (2013) and McNutt (2014) characterize as risk intolerant and favoring convention. By training diplomats, formulating guidelines and developing best practices, MFAs may be attempting to manage the risk associated with online activity.

In summary, the findings presented thus far suggest that MFAs have indeed institutionalized digital diplomacy, thereby offering an answer to this study's first research question.

This study's second research question evaluated MFAs' ability to reap the benefits of incorporating social media in the practice of diplomacy. While the MFAs evaluated in this study have all migrated online, their digital diplomacy models varied greatly with regard to supervision of online activity at the MFA and embassy levels. Such models seem to be situated along a "supervision axis" that ranges from rigorous to lax supervision. Poland was the most rigorous MFA, as all content published online must be approved by department heads or ambassadors. This model was characterized as "train and supervise." The most lax ministry was the Finish MFA, which has adopted a model of "train, trust and provide," where missions' online activity is rarely monitored. Israel's model includes more rigorous supervision when compared to Norway's lax model, which supervises missions that have just recently migrated online. As Khatib, Dutton and Thelwall (2012) argue, while rigorous supervision models reduce possible loss of control over the communication process, they also prevent MFAs from practicing real-time diplomacy (Seib, 2012) or engaging in dialogue as replies to followers must first be approved.

The Arab Spring was one of the main drivers of digital diplomacy, as nations realized the need to monitor the social media ecology (Seib, 2012). This study finds that MFAs have yet to realize the potential of SNS as a source of valuable information to foreign policy makers. With the exception of Norway's MFA, digital diplomacy staffers do not monitor online content authored by foreign MFAs or news outlets nor do they transmit such information to relevant departments. Similarly, embassy managers do not gather online information from local SNS. By failing to communicate discussions taking place on local SNS to the MFA, embassies prevent their ministries from listening to foreign publics and tailoring foreign policy accordingly (Metzgar, 2012). These findings are in contrast to Causey and Howard's (2013) assertion that monitoring social media is now an integral part of the diplomatic toolkit.

This important finding may be linked to the identity of digital diplomacy practitioners at both the ministry and embassy level. Social media and communications experts at the ministry level, as well as local employees at the embassy level, may lack the skills necessary to identify information pertinent to policy makers. Thus, utilizing SNS as an information source may require that MFAs incorporate more career diplomats in digital diplomacy or communications units.

There are two additional findings with regard to information gathering that warrant further elaboration. The first was a statement made by the head of the Polish digital diplomacy division, which indicated that embassies may have yet to exploit SNS as an information source, as ambassadors still focus on traditional media such as newspapers and TV. This statement echoes Vance's findings (2012) and further illustrates ambassadors' role as digital gatekeepers.

Interestingly, Norway's MFA encourages its ambassadors to use SNS as an information source, even if they themselves do not publish content on these platforms. Essentially, Norway's MFA has transformed diplomats into SNS lurkers. This finding suggests that diplomatic institutions may reach a more important audience than they realize, as some diplomats lurk in the shadows. This finding also supports the US Digital Outreach Team's assertion that online engagement reaches a large audience, as it includes lurkers who view the communication process without partaking in it (Khatib, Dutton & Thelwall, 2012).

Secondly, Metzgar (2012) states that digital diplomacy enables MFAs to increase the relevance of their content by tailoring it to the language, culture and values of online followers. The majority of embassy level managers at the Polish, Israeli and Finnish MFAs indicated that they use follower feedback (e.g., shares, re-tweets) in order to create content that is relevant to their audiences. Likewise, the majority of embassy level managers stated that they adapt MFA-authored content to the culture, interests and language of their followers. Such activities indicate that embassy managers do indeed practice tailoring, which may constitute a form of information gathering because followers' opinions are taken into account in the communication process.

Similar to Harris (2013) and Stein (2011), the results of this study suggest that MFAs now routinely use SNS and websites to manage their national image. Indeed, the practice of selfie diplomacy was an integral part of MFA and embassy level digital diplomacy activity in the Polish, Finnish and Israeli MFAs. Currently, selfie diplomacy seems to focus on scientific, technological and cultural achievements, as well as the promotion of tourism and investments. As such, nation branding through social media remains focused on the projection of a positive national image (Harris, 2013) and is financially motivated (Manor & Segev, 2015).

MFAs in the sample also realized the potential of SNS to author and frame their national narrative and image (Natarajan, 2014). In Poland's case, such framing deals mainly with the nation's history and Nazi concentration camps operated on Polish soil. At a time when images rule supreme, a nation's history may indeed be as relevant as a nation's present. Yet Poland's focus on its past may also be demonstrative of Van Ham's concept of social power (2013), in which nations adhere to established values. Poland's focus on re-branding its past may thus be viewed as an attempt to associate its brand with the desirable values of cultural diversity and celebration of minorities, as opposed to the violent oppression of minorities. Whilst Poland focuses on its past, Israel frames its present while also adhering to accepted values such as the celebration of cultural, rather than military, achievements and the promotion of "green" technological solutions meant to tackle climate change.

National images are an important facet of diplomatic activity, as they contribute to a nation's financial prosperity, enable nations to promote their foreign policy among the international community and impact the willingness of populations to support another nation's foreign policy (Quelch & Jocz, 2009; Manor & Segev, 2015). However, this study finds that MFAs dedicate ever growing resources to managing their image. While Poland's MFA has a unit dedicated solely to nation branding, Finland dedicates all its online activity to the "This is Finland" campaign. Likewise, all Israeli SNS channels include nation-branding content. It is therefore possible that we are witnessing a shift in which branding becomes the focus of diplomatic activities and in which image trumps policy and selfies outweigh the self.

When evaluating public diplomacy at the MFA level, three findings are of special significance. First, MFAs seem to use different SNS for different goals. Three of the four MFAs evaluated in this study used Twitter for political communication with elites, while Facebook was used for nation branding activities and reaching foreign populations. This use of SNS may be regarded as a form of tailoring, as MFAs identify the platforms with which to reach specific audiences (Xiguang & Jing, 2010; Archetti, 2012).

Secondly, like Archetti (2012) and Bjola and Jiang (2015), this study found that MFAs tend to value elite audiences (e.g., journalists, opinion makers) over foreign populations. Targeting of elites may indicate that MFAs still adhere to Entman's framing model in which governmental policies must be passed down a cascade that begins with the newsroom elite and ends with the public (Entman, 2003). Yet Entman's is a web 1.0 model that does not include the web 2.0 features of direct communication with, and feedback from, SNS followers. The lack of focus on foreign populations could indicate that MFAs use online platforms mainly for message dissemination among the newsroom elite. This may be a result of the fact that digital diplomacy units are staffed, and often managed, by former journalists who still regard the media as an information gatekeeper.

Additionally, MFA press spokespersons were traditionally tasked with issuing ongoing press releases. It is therefore possible that situating digital diplomacy activity in spokesperson's departments leads to the utilization of social media for one-way message dissemination. Finally, it is also possible that diplomats still regard traditional mass media as the most effective public diplomacy medium given an ability to reach vast audiences (Vance, 2012).

Interestingly, no MFA or embassy level digital diplomacy mangers stated that their online activity targets citizen journalists. Studies have shown that these have risen to the position of information gatekeepers (Meraz & Papacharissi, 2013) and now influence the framing of events and issues (Stein, 2011). The fact that MFAs have yet to target citizen journalists furthers the assumption that they still adhere to Entman's model, created in a time of newsroom elite hegemony.

The third finding deals with MFAs' communication goals. When foreign populations were identified as an important public diplomacy audience, the issue of *influence* took center stage. While MFAs such as Finland and Israel use numerous languages in an attempt to reach foreign populations (e.g., Russian, Chinese), the goal of such communication remains the "winning of hearts and minds." Thus, public diplomacy may still be dominated by the notion of *influencing* foreign populations rather than fostering relationships with them. By aspiring to influence followers, rather than listen to them, MFAs disregard the ethical dimension of two-way symmetrical communication in which the goal of dialogue is dialogue itself (Fitzpatrick, 2007; Brown, 2013) as both the organization and the individual seek to form mutually beneficial relationships (Kent & Taylor, 1998; Vance, 2012). In fact, the art of influence may have even become more sophisticated, given MFAs' very use of SNS, which portrays a commitment to genuine dialogue (Taylor, 2007). Yet influence still runs counter to SNS followers' premium on trust and sincerity (Seo & Kinsey, 2013).

It should be noted that Israel's use of SNS channels in Arabic and Persian may constitute an attempt to use digital diplomacy to overcome the limitations of traditional diplomacy as most of the Arab world, and Iran, have yet to establish diplomatic relations with Israel. Further analysis is warranted in order to ascertain if Israel's MFA does indeed engage in dialogue with its Arab followers, thus differing from Virtual Embassy Tehran (Metzgar, 2012), and whether it creates collaborative opportunities as was the case with Second House of Sweden (Pamment, 2013).

In contrast to MFA staffers, the embassy level digital diplomacy managers mentioned the local population as an important target audience. This finding might suggest that MFAs use social media for global message dissemination while embassies practice public diplomacy by communicating with online publics. An interesting difference was found between the Israeli and Polish embassy level managers. While Polish managers tended to list the local population as the last audience targeted in their online activity, Israeli managers listed them first. This may indicate that MFAs place different emphases on communicating with foreign populations and that the practice of digital diplomacy is evolving at different paces within different diplomatic institutions.

This study found that both MFAs and embassies dedicate resources to communicating with their domestic populations (e.g., Polish MFA targets Polish citizens) and national diasporas, a finding which is consistent with Cha, Yeo & Kim's (2014) evaluation of the online activity of embassies in South Korea. The focus on communication with one's domestic population, and providing it with consular aid, may reflect an attempt by MFAs to create their own constituency even though they face the world with their backs to the nation (Copeland, 2013). Developing a constituency may enable MFAs to safeguard their role and resources within government in an age of whole-of-government approaches to diplomacy (Golberg & Kaduck, 2011).

The interview with Norway's press officer coincided with the 2015 earthquake in Nepal. According to the press officer, embassies near Nepal were following special guidelines created by the MFA regarding the use of SNS in times of crisis. In adherence to these guidelines, embassies were collecting relevant information from citizens and local SNS and transmitting them to the MFA which, in turn, used embassies' SNS in order to coordinate aid. These findings suggest that MFAs have realized the potential of using SNS to coordinate consular activity and gather information in times of crisis (Harris, 2013; Kampf, Manor & Segev, 2015). Likewise, crisis communication may be one area of activity in which the practice of real-time diplomacy is most evident (Seib, 2012).

Maintaining ties with diasporas may represent a "connective mindshift" among MFAs who now practice networked diplomacy in an attempt to utilize their diasporas as a national resource (Zaharna, Arsenalut & Fisher, 2013). A networked mentality was also evident among the Polish, Israeli and Finnish MFAs, who use their embassies to manage global nation branding and policy oriented campaigns (e.g., "This is Finland," the fight against terror). By so doing, MFAs conceptualize their online presence as a global information network.

As opposed to the development of network mentalities, the actual practice of networked diplomacy, explored through the use of languages, offered conflicting results. Poland's MFA seems to have realized that its embassies are part of a multitude of intersecting online social networks, each with a different focus and each necessitating a different language. Polish embassies publish online content in Polish, as they are part of the social network of the Polish MFA in which information flows from the hub (i.e., MFA) to the periphery (i.e., embassies) and vice versa. Likewise, Polish embassies are part of a social network of Polish citizens interested in foreign policy. These embassies also publish content in English because they are part of the social network of embassies in a host nation, and in the local language as they are part of their own social network which includes the local population. As opposed to Polish embassies, Norwegian and Israeli embassies publish online content solely in local languages (e.g., Spanish in Spain) thereby limiting their ability to interact with the diplomatic milieu, their domestic audience and their MFA. These findings again suggest that digital diplomacy evolves at different paces in different MFAs.

Anne-Marie Slaughter has argued that networked diplomacy achieves diplomatic goals by bringing together governments, corporations, organizations and individuals (2009). NGOs are of special importance to the practice of networked diplomacy, given their ability to impact decision making at various levels of government (Copeland, 2013; Corrie, 2015). Interestingly, NGOs were only mentioned by two embassy level managers. Likewise, the Norwegian press officer was the only interviewee who addressed the impact NGOs have had on diplomacy. Remarkably, his comments did not focus on collaborating with NGOs but rather on the MFA's decision not to interact with single-issue NGOs that may criticize aspects of Norwegian foreign policy. Thus, this study finds that non-state actors have yet to rise in importance among the practitioners of digital diplomacy. As such, it furthers Clarke's (2015) assertion that while MFA communication is networked, it is state-centric.

In summary, the findings presented in this section do not offer a definitive answer with regard to MFAs' ability to reap the benefits of social media. While MFAs and embassies do tailor SNS content, offer consular aid in times of crisis through social media, use SNS to overcome the limitations of traditional diplomacy and manage their national image, their activity is still focused on influencing foreign populations and the newsroom elite while failing to collaborate with non-state actors and gather relevant information from SNS. These mixed results further the assumption that the practice of digital diplomacy is still evolving as MFAs continue to master its practice.

The final research question posed by this study analyzed MFAs' ability to overcome the challenges of integrating social media into the practice of diplomacy. While this study found that MFAs now offer social media training to diplomats, it also identified generational gaps between digital natives and digital immigrants (Presnky, 2001). These gaps were made apparent through the diversity in the ages of embassy level digital diplomacy managers. In all MFAs evaluated, digital natives relied less on MFA-authored content when compared to digital immigrants. Digital natives were also more likely to use their MFA's SNS accounts in order to identify ministry priorities, while immigrants relied mostly on official communication with the MFA. Additionally, digital natives used follower feedback (e.g., number of shares) to author more appealing content while immigrants used such feedback to identify instances of loss of control over the communication process. Lastly, natives were more likely to include elements of a web 2.0 ethos in their definitions of engagement (McNutt, 2014).

The aforementioned gaps suggest that MFAs have yet to face the challenge of narrowing conceptual and operational gaps between digital natives and immigrants which may substantially influence an embassy's ability to practice digital diplomacy. Such gaps may also inhibit ambassadors, who are likely to be digital immigrants, from embracing social media activity. These gaps also suggest that embassies in which digital diplomacy is managed by an immigrant require closer guidance and more substantial content from the ministry. Finally, MFAs do not seem to train staffers at both the ministry and embassy level in digital diplomacy literacy. This finding may explain the overall lack of use of SNS as an information source observed in this study as those who monitor SNS may not be able to decipher all information coded into a 140-character tweet.

Rigorous supervision models may inhibit an MFA's ability to practice real-time diplomacy as events are likely to outpace the supervision process, rendering MFAs irrelevant. While supervision hinders real-time diplomacy, autonomy facilitates it. Thus, an important finding is the overall sense of autonomy expressed by the majority of embassy level managers. While these reported to career diplomats and were monitored by the MFA, they still expressed their autonomy with regard to phrasing of online content, issues to be addressed and use of multi-media. It is this autonomy that may enable embassies to react in near real time to events taking place in host countries. Therefore, this study identifies two components that may be necessary to meet the challenge of real-time diplomacy: relatively lax supervision and increased sense of autonomy among embassy digital diplomacy managers.

The embassies' growing autonomy may also reflect recognition by MFAs that one cannot manage global media empires while controlling all messages disseminated across all channels. If this is indeed the case, then MFAs may be slowly relinquishing control over the communication process and adapting to a risk-prone environment (Copeland, 2013; McNutt, 2014). MFAs' willingness to increase embassy autonomy may also suggest that ministries have realized that ours is a sharing society in which people expect governments to share information with them (Wichowski, 2015).

The majority of embassy digital diplomacy managers stated that less than 10% of all content they publish online is derived from the ministry, while the remainder is derived from embassy personnel. However, results indicate that the degree of such embassy-wide collaboration varies greatly between MFAs and between embassies within an MFA. In the Polish MFA, embassy managers rarely receive information from colleagues, while in Finland and Norway's case the majority of managers both participate in weekly embassy meetings and regularly receive information from their colleagues. These findings illustrate the need for embassy-wide collaboration in the authoring of SNS content. If it takes a village to raise a child, it takes an embassy to practice digital diplomacy. These findings also further the argument that ambassadors are digital gatekeepers, as they oversee embassy-wide collaborations.

While MFAs author online content that narrates their national image, they are by no means the only governmental ministry to do so. When evaluating the challenge of plurality of online channels, this study offers conflicting results. Several interviewees stated that plurality of online channels does not constitute a major challenge to MFA activity. In Poland there is actually a deficit in official SNS channels in English. In Norway's case, the director of the press office stated that coordination of online content occurs on an ad hoc basis but is usually unnecessary, as the MFA "knows where its responsibility ends." While this may be true, lack of coordination of online content within government may impair the MFA's ability to illustrate a nation's image, author a consistent foreign policy and narrate a coherent national narrative (Natarajan, 2014). This is especially true in nations that have adopted a whole-of-government approach to diplomacy (Golberg & Kaduck, 2011) or nations that have traditionally segmented their public diplomacy efforts. Such is the case with Israel which at one time created a unique "national public diplomacy forum" meant to coordinate all Israeli public diplomacy activity (Molad, 2012). Interestingly, in Israel one finds plurality of channels both within the government and within the MFA itself as the Cultural and Economic departments operate their own SNS channels. This study found little coordination between Israeli governmental ministries and within the MFA. Likewise, while the Finnish ministry closely coordinates its online nation branding activities with other ministries, there is no coordination on foreign policy issues. It therefore seems that while the digital age has challenged the MFA's position as a national narrator, this challenge remains unaddressed by MFAs.

All MFAs evaluated in this study now operate social media empires spanning hundreds of SNS accounts (e.g., Twitter, Facebook, Weibo), websites and blogs. MFA presence on numerous SNS may constitute an attempt to communicate with a global public sphere fragmented to networks of selective exposure (Hayden, 2012). However, continuously creating new content for such empires, and interacting with followers, calls into question the economic feasibility of digital diplomacy once believed to be "cost effective" diplomacy

(Archetti, 2012; Copeland, 2013). As an Israeli MFA staffer indicated, identical content soon finds its way across all MFA platforms due to limited resources. Lack of resources was also identified as a challenge by all interviewees given that MFAs operate in a 24-hour-news cycle and amid growing competition over followers from other MFAs and news outlets (Hayden, 2012).

Williamson and Kelly (2012) state that virtual spaces are now collaborative spaces in which digital diplomacy followers express their sense of agency. As Kampf, Manor & Segev (2015) argue, by neglecting to create collaborative opportunities MFAs may fail to meet the expectations of followers, thereby driving them away or diminishing their willingness to engage in dialogue. Notably, of all participants in this study, only one embassy level manager stated that she creates collaborative opportunities in which followers co-create content with the embassy. Thus, the participatory dimension of digital diplomacy identified by Zaharna and Rugh (2012) has failed to materialize among the MFAs in this study. Such lack of collaborative opportunities may also prevent followers from becoming advocates of MFAs in peer-to-peer diplomacy (Attias, 2012; Saunders, 2013), limiting ministries' ability to reach diverse spheres of influence.

The emergence of the "new" public diplomacy represented a conceptual shift which called on nations to engage with connected publics and create relationships with them (Cull, 2008; Meissen, 2005; Hayden, 2012). This was to be achieved by transitioning from one-way flows of information to two-way dialogical and collaborative forms of engagement (Pamment, 2013; McNutt, 2014). As relationships are the foundation of SNS (Waters et al., 2009) these were viewed as pivotal tools in the practice of the "new" public diplomacy (Archetti, 2012). Thus, one of the most significant findings of this study is the overall lack of engagement and dialogue with online publics.

Indeed, the results of this study suggest that the conceptual shift of the "new" public diplomacy has yet to translate into a practical one. Three of the four MFAs evaluated in this study stated that two-way dialogic engagement with online followers was a rare occurrence and was not the focus of their online activity. In the Polish case, public engagement seems to be limited to information dissemination while Finland solely focuses on correcting false information disseminated online. Ongoing dialogue and creation of relationships with foreign populations has yet to become a staple of these MFAs' online activity. Similarly, the majority of embassy level managers also stated that actual engagement was a rarity. This finding is somewhat contradictory to Arachetti's (2012) assertion that embassies utilize new technologies for public engagement because of a reduction in their informational and representational capacities.

Interviewees offered two explanations for lack of dialogue with followers. The first is MFAs' risk-averse culture, which still treats social media with suspicion. This finding lends credence to Kampf, Manor & Segev's (2015) assertion that MFAs employ a web 1.0 mentality in web 2.0 environments. Secondly, Polish, Norwegian and Finnish interviewees all stated that online followers are not keen on engaging in dialogue with MFAs. This finding contradicts the most basic assumption of the relational approach to public diplomacy, according to which foreign populations are willing to engage in dialogue with MFAs—thus facilitating the creation of relationships (Gregory, 2011; Seo, 2013). Likewise, the premise of the "new" public diplomacy rests on two-way communication models in which MFAs and publics converse on matters of shared interest (Cowan & Arsenault, 2008). Yet if online publics do not seek engagement, it means that dialogue, let alone relationships, cannot be formed.

However, it is possible that this finding is linked to MFAs' unwillingness to engage with critics of their country. With the exception of Israel, MFAs in the sample seem to view critics as potential hazards at best and trolls spamming their accounts at worst. Although trolls do indeed exist, not every form of criticism constitutes an attack on the state. In fact, critics who take time to respond to MFA-authored content may be the very audience seeking engagement and dialogue, given their desire to voice their opinions. The Norwegian ministry's policy of not engaging with expressions of opinions prevents it from reaching, and possibly altering the position of, its harshest critics. Thus, one may claim that engagement with critics is the very essence of the "new" public diplomacy and that these MFAs simply do not practice it. Moreover, the parameters used by MFAs to evaluate public diplomacy dealt primarily with reach of content rather than scope of dialogue. Dialogue is thus not only avoided, it is not measured.

Embassy level managers often reflected their MFA's attitude towards engagement in dialogue as a whole, and engaging with critics in particular. While Finnish embassy managers mentioned dialogue in their definition of engagement, they also stated that they only rarely receive questions from online followers. A similar sentiment was expressed by Norwegian embassy managers who stated that actual engagement was a rare occurrence and they are not presented with many opportunities to engage with followers. However, as was the case with their MFAs, Norwegian and Finnish embassy managers also stated that they do not engage with critics. Israeli embassy managers all stated that dialogue was an important factor of the term "engagement." However, these managers only engage with people who do not pre-judge Israel. Finally, when asked which parameters are used to assess public engagement, the majority of all embassy managers identified parameters that evaluate reach of content rather than scope of dialogue.

The lack of online public engagement and use of SNS for monologic communication found in this study echoes the findings of Manor, Kampf & Segev (2015) and Bjola and Jiang (2015). In this regard, this study further solidifies the claim that MFAs have yet to realize the potential of SNS to create long-term relationships with foreign populations through online dialogue. However, one cannot disregard the sentiment expressed by the majority of MFA interviewees, and embassy managers, regarding followers' lack of willingness to engage in dialogue with diplomatic institutions. It is this sentiment that leads the researcher to conclude that both diplomatic institutions and their online followers are still adapting to web 2.0 environments and negotiating their respective roles in the online communication process. While MFAs and embassies are still cautious in their use of social media, SNS followers appear to offer limited opportunities for dialogic engagement. This conclusion differs from those reached in previous studies that have focused solely on MFAs' lack of engagement with followers without taking into account followers' willingness to engage with diplomatic institutions (Bjola & Jiang, 2015; Kampf, Manor & Segev, 2015). Thus, this finding constitutes the study's main contribution to the digital diplomacy research corpus.

In response to the third research question posed by this study, results indicate that MFAs have been able to address several of the challenges brought about by their migration online including relinquishing some control over the communication process, adapting to a sharing society and practicing near real-time diplomacy. However, challenges such as plurality of channels and reducing gaps between digital natives and immigrants have yet to be met. Most importantly, the transition towards collaborative, networked and dialogic public diplomacy has yet to take root. Zhang argues that symmetrical communication is more than just dialogue, but presently MFAs seem to communicate just in monologues (Zhang, 2013).

The three research questions employed in this study enable it to reflect on how MFAs vary in their use of social media and what explains this variance. First, this study finds that variance in digital diplomacy practice arises from the fact that it is evolving at different paces within different MFAs. While some MFAs seem to employ lax supervision models and offer diplomats autonomy in the creation of online content, others are more cautious in their use of SNS. Likewise, while some MFAs use numerous languages online and adopt a networked mentality, others limit online activity to domestic and local languages.

Secondly, MFAs differ in the goals they aim to achieve through the use of SNS. While Israel aims to use SNS to foster dialogue with populations in

Arab countries and overcome the limitations of traditional public diplomacy, Finland focuses its efforts solely on nation branding activities. Such differences lead to different online strategies, such as the use of two-way dialogue versus dissemination of information regarding national achievements and investment opportunities. It is therefore evident that MFAs cannot be regarded as one monolithic unit and that digital diplomacy studies must abandon "one size fits all" evaluations and recommendations.

Likewise, MFA informational objectives also contribute to variance in the usage of social media. For instance, MFAs that value message dissemination may choose to publish identical content on numerus platforms as a means to reach the largest possible audience. MFAs that attempt to form online relationships may use different SNS to reach different audiences, such as sharing different content on each platform.

Third, variance in MFA usage of social media arises from the manner in which MFAs collaborate with outside parties such as NGOs and other ministries. Some MFAs regard NGOs as a possible threat to their status, while others view them as an important target audience for online activity. Likewise, some MFAs operate in governments that have adopted whole-of-government approaches to diplomacy, while other governments work in silos. Variance in relationships with outside parties thus leads to variance in use of SNS.

Finally, variance in usage of SNS also arises from internal working routines. In some MFAs, the department in charge of online communication oversees all online activity including publication of content on SNS. Other MFAs allow ministerial departments to manage their own respective social media accounts (e.g., economic department, cultural department). When internal departments manage their own accounts, they may be able to use SNS as a source of information for policy makers. On the other hand, MFA-wide collaboration and the authoring of a coherent national image may be hindered.

Through its analysis of embassy usage of SNS, this study also offers insight into how embassies vary in their use of SNS both within and between MFAs. Variance in embassy usage of social media seems to arise from four factors. First, and most important, is the manner in which the local ambassador views social media and its ability to further diplomatic goals. Ambassadors who view social media as an important diplomatic tool are more likely to encourage online activity and include embassy level digital diplomacy managers in embassy-wide meetings or projects. Secondly, variance arises from the identity of the embassy level digital diplomacy manager. Digital natives are more likely to tailor SNS content and engage in dialogue—as opposed to immigrants, who are more cautious in their use of SNS. Likewise, trained diplomats are more likely to engage online with critics than local employees.

Third, resources account for embassy variance. In larger embassies, digital diplomacy activity is undertaken by a seasoned and trained diplomat, as opposed to a part-time local employee in smaller embassies. Dedicated digital diplomacy staff is necessary for an embassy to create engaging content and form online relationships with followers. Finally, training and communication with the MFA also accounts for variance in social media usage at the embassy level. Training is paramount for embassy level online activity, as the use of social media for diplomatic goals is a craft. Only one MFA in this study, Israel, convenes all embassy level managers for specialized training seminars. Communication between the MFA and embassies also varies, as some ministries offer ongoing council and assistance with content formulation while others simply check for inaccuracies. Given the need to continuously author engaging content, embassy level activity is dependent upon MFA content, information and media.

In conclusion, this study finds that MFAs have yet to realize the potential of digital diplomacy. Findings also suggest that digital diplomacy remains an evolution, not a revolution, in the practice of diplomacy. Social media tools are currently used to enhance MFA abilities rather than create new ones. Through online content (i.e., SNS and websites), MFAs easily and immediately disseminate information to newsroom elites, foreign diplomatic institutions and foreign populations. However, while MFA content now reaches a global audience, this audience is still viewed as passive rather than proactive, and the goal of such communication remains influence (Zaharna, Arsenault & Fisher, 2013). Thus, the effects of social media on the practice of diplomacy are mostly temporal and spatial and are therefore similar to those brought on by the telegraph, radio and television. The "new" public diplomacy has yet to fully materialize on the Twitter channels and Facebook profiles of embassies throughout the world and two-way communication remains an elusive goal, both for MFAs and their followers. A true revolution in diplomacy would see both a conceptual and practical shift in public diplomacy. Conceptual, as the goal of online activity would no longer be *influence* but rather symmetrical, ethical dialogue in which followers are provided with information given a desire to interact with a knowledgeable partner (Kent & Taylor, 1998). Practical, in the sense that MFAs would dedicate the resources necessary for continuous dialogic engagement with followers.

This study found that MFAs seem to use their migration online to improve their standing within government by creating a domestic constituency. Therefore, much of digital diplomacy is domestic diplomacy. On the other hand, the increasing autonomy of embassies suggests that power is migrating from the hub (MFA) to the periphery (embassies). These contradictory and multi-directional shifts in power are emblematic of the networked age, in which networks challenge the hierarchal structure of institutions (Hocking & Melissen, 2015).

Finally, it is important to note this study's limitations. First, the use of qualitative research tools (i.e., interviews, questionnaires) coupled with the size and homogenous nature of this study's sample, preclude the generalization of findings beyond mid-sized Western MFAs. Secondly, the use of questionnaires to evaluate embassy level digital diplomacy, as opposed to interviews, may have precluded respondents from offering lengthy answers that would have provided greater insight. Another limitation stems from the fact that respondents were often local employees who may have had difficulty completing questionnaires in English. The use of questionnaires may have also prevented the researcher from fully understanding the manner in which embassy level managers define and imagine digital diplomacy, thus running counter to this study's constitutive approach.

Third, as MFAs were asked to select embassies that are active on social media, it is possible that the results of the questionnaires' analysis are relevant only to those embassies, as other missions are less active online. Moreover, the timing of the interviews with MFA digital diplomacy practitioners may have also impacted this study's results. As the interview with Norway's press officer was held during the crisis in Nepal, he was able to expand on his MFA's use of SNS in times of crisis, while this issue was not fully addressed in other interviews taking place before this event. Fourth, this study focused solely on the use of social media in the practice of diplomacy. Yet the concept of digital diplomacy is much broader and includes a variety of technologies (e.g., email) and ICTs (e.g., smartphone). Each of these technologies is accompanied by unique challenges and benefits, which may differ from those associated with social media.

In addition, while this study found that MFAs offer diplomats social media training, it did not elaborate on this important aspect. As training is a prerequisite for digital diplomacy activity, and as training may account for variance in MFA and embassy usage of SNS, there is a need to more thoroughly investigate MFA social media training. Such an investigation should explore the tools and skills developed during training sessions and the extent to which diplomats implement lessons learned. Moreover, some MFAs indicated that the digital diplomacy activity of diplomats and embassies is evaluated yearly. Future studies should analyze items such as evaluations as a stepping stone toward understanding MFA goals in using social media and adopted strategies.

Given its constitutive approach, this study offers a snapshot of the practice of digital diplomacy. Yet as this practice is still evolving, there is a need for ongoing evaluations of digital diplomacy activity at both the ministry and embassy level. It may therefore be incumbent on digital diplomacy scholars to adopt the methodology of longitudinal studies, thereby charting the progression of digital diplomacy practice.

Another limitation of this study deals with the concept of digital diplomacy literacy. While this concept was introduced in this study, it warrants further elaboration, as there is a need to more clearly articulate what skills and competencies comprise this term. Likewise, there is a need to evaluate whether digital diplomacy practitioners have developed such skills and if digital natives more easily develop digital diplomacy literacy given their familiarity with online environments and digital tools. Future studies should test this hypothesis, which has implications for MFA training and allocation of resources.

Lastly, as this study attempted to address both the challenges and benefits of digital diplomacy, it offers a broad overview of the practice of digital diplomacy rather than an in-depth analysis of each challenge and benefit identified in the literature review.

As digital diplomacy is a global phenomenon, future studies should evaluate the incorporation of social media in larger and more diverse MFAs (e.g., Arab or Asian MFAs). There is also a need to investigate the effect social media has had on multi-lateral organizations that are part of the diplomatic community (e.g., UN, OSCE). It is also imperative to understand the motivation of individuals following MFAs on social media as well as their interests and expectations from online engagement. While this study focused on the perceptions, experiences and insights of digital diplomacy practitioners, it is also necessary to analyze the content shared by MFAs online as well their attempts to stimulate dialogue and create participatory opportunities.

Conclusion

Alexander Wendt has argued that International Relations scholarship would benefit from the adoption of both causal and constitutive theoretical approaches (Wendt, 1998). This is a result of the fact that unlike natural sciences, IR deals with social systems and social agents. Indeed diplomacy itself is a social institution which influences, and is influenced by, the society in which it operates. The fact that modern society migrated *en masse* to the online world prompted MFAs to follow suit, giving birth to digital diplomacy.

This study adopted a constitutive approach to digital diplomacy given the fact that, before this form of diplomacy may be practiced, it must first be imagined and conceptualized by diplomats. This theoretical approach holds relevance to IR scholarship as a whole since it recognizes the uniqueness of social agents and the systems in which they operate. As such, this study asserts that each MFA is a world unto itself consisting of its own organizational culture, mentality, status within government and goals. What follows is that digital diplomacy studies can no longer treat foreign ministries as a monolithic unit employing identical strategies and adopting similar practices. Comparative studies, and cross-national comparisons, are one way to cope with this reality.

Within the narrower field of nation branding and public diplomacy scholarship, this study contributes to the existing research corpus by diversifying its units of analysis. All four MFAs evaluated in this study were neglected by previous studies using an American-centric approach to public diplomacy research. The migration of MFAs to social media is a truly global phenomenon, and across Africa, Latin America and Asia, foreign ministries are advancing its practice. Digital diplomacy scholarship must therefore continuously extend its reach to diverse geographic regions.

Within the even narrower field of digital diplomacy scholarship, this study posits that digital diplomacy is now fully integrated into all aspects of diplomatic practice ranging from public affairs and nation branding to public diplomacy and advocacy campaigns. Therefore, it offers a new narrative for the emergence of digital diplomacy that transcends silos and focuses on the benefits and challenges brought about by the incorporation of social media and SNS in the practice of diplomacy.

The results of this study suggest that digital diplomacy is still evolving. Moreover, it appears to be evolving at different paces within different MFAs. Several factors were identified as contributing to variance in social media use between MFAs. First was the supervision model employed by foreign ministries, which may inhibit or facilitate the migration of diplomats online. Second, use of languages at both the MFA and embassy levels influences the audiences that may be targeted through social media. Third, the goals of social media use influence its implementation (i.e., public diplomacy versus nation branding). Finally, working routines within MFAs, resources, and relationships with external agents (e.g., NGOs, other government ministries) also contribute to variance in social media use.

At the embassy level, three factors were identified as contributing to variance in social media use: the importance assigned to digital diplomacy activity by the Ambassador; the identity of embassy-level digital diplomacy managers (i.e., digital natives, digital immigrants); and resources made available to embassy managers.

Notably, the main limitation of this study is its focus on social media and SNS while digital diplomacy far exceeds these tools. UN Ambassadors are now using smartphones in order to relay information in real time to their ministries. Embassies have adopted smartphone applications such as WhatsApp to manage consular crises while foreign ministries are utilizing new analytical tools to evaluate their online reach. Each of these tools is influencing the craft of diplomacy and warrants further investigation. Thus far, we have only begun to scratch the surface of the phenomenon called digital diplomacy.

Bibliography

Abbasi, M. A., Kumar, S., Andrade Filho, J. A., & Liu, H. (2012). Lessons Learned in Using Social Media for Disaster Relief-ASU Crisis Response Game. In *Social Computing, Behavioral-Cultural Modeling and Prediction* (pp. 282–89). Springer Berlin Heidelberg.

Al-Saggaf, Y., & Williamson, K. (2004, September). Online Communities in Saudi Arabia: Evaluating the Impact on Culture Through Online Semi-structured Interviews. In *Forum Qualitative Sozialforschung/Forum: Qualitative Social Research* (Vol. 5, No. 3).

Archetti, C. (2012). The Impact of New Media on Diplomatic Practice: An Evolutionary Model of Change. *The Hague Journal of Diplomacy, 7*(2), 181–206.

Attias, S. (2012). Israel's New Peer-to-peer Diplomacy. *The Hague Journal of Diplomacy, 7*(4), 473–82.

Bélanger, F., & Carter, L. (2008). Trust and Risk in E-government Adoption. *The Journal of Strategic Information Systems, 17*(2), 165–76.

Bjola, C. (2014). The Ethics of Secret Diplomacy: A Contextual Approach. *Journal of Global Ethics, 10*(1), 85–100.

Bjola, C., & Holmes, M. (2015). *Digital Diplomacy: Theory and Practice*. New York: Routledge.

Bjola, C., & Jiang, L. (2015). Social Media and Public Diplomacy: A Comparative Analysis of the Digital Diplomatic Strategies of the EU, US and Japan in China. In C. Bjola and M. Holmes (Eds.), *Digital Diplomacy Theory and Practice* (pp. 71–88). Oxon: Routledge.

Bortree, D. S., & Seltzer, T. (2009). Dialogic Strategies and Outcomes: An Analysis of Environmental Advocacy Groups' Facebook Profiles. *Public Relations Review, 35*(3), 317–19.

Boyd, D., & Ellison, N. (2007). Social Network Sites: Definition, History, and Scholarship. *Journal of Computer-Mediated Communication, 13*(1), 210–30.

Britten, N. (1995). Qualitative Interviews in Medical Research. *BMJ: British Medical Journal, 311*(6999), 251.

Brown, R. (2013). The Politics of Relational Public Diplomacy. In R. S. Zaharna, A. Arsenault & A. Fisher (Eds.), *Relational, Networked and Collaborative Approaches to Public Diplomacy: The Connective Mindshift* (pp. 44–55). Oxon: Routledge.

Castells, M. (2011). *The Rise of the Network Society: The Information Age: Economy, Society, and culture* (Vol. 1). John Wiley & Sons.

Causey, C., & Howard, P. N. (2013). Delivering Digital Public Diplomacy. In R. S. Zaharna, A. Arsenault & A. Fisher (Eds.), *Relational, Networked and Collaborative Approaches to Public Diplomacy: The Connective Mindshift* (pp. 144–56). Oxon: Routledge.

Cha, H., Yeo, S., & Kim, B. (2014). Social Media's Dialogic Communication of Foreign Embassies in Korea and Public Diplomacy: Based on Dialogic Communication Theory.

Clarke, A. (2015). Business as Usual? An Evolution of British and Canadian Digital Diplomacy as Policy Change. In C. Bjola and M. Holmes (Eds.), *Digital Diplomacy Theory and Practice* (pp. 111–26). Oxon: Routledge.

Comor, E., & Bean, H. (2012). America's 'Engagement' Delusion: Critiquing a Public Diplomacy Consensus. *International Communication Gazette, 74*(3), 203–20.

Comor, E. (2013). Digital Engagement: America's Use (and Misuse) of Marshall McLuhan. *New Political Science, 35*(1), 1–18.

Copeland, D. (2013). Taking Diplomacy Public. In R. S. Zaharna, A. Arsenault & A. Fisher (Eds.), *Relational, Networked and Collaborative Approaches to Public Diplomacy: The Connective Mindshift* (pp. 56–69). Oxon: Routledge.

Corrie, K. L. (2015). The International Criminal Court: Using Technology in Network Diplomacy. In C. Bjola and M. Holmes (Eds.), *Digital Diplomacy Theory and Practice* (pp. 145–63). Oxon: Routledge.

Cowan, G., Arsenault, A. (2008). Moving from Monologue to Dialogue to Collaboration: The Three Layer of Public Diplomacy. *The ANNALS of the American Academy of Political and Social Science, 616*(1), 10–30.

Cull, N. J. (2008). Public Diplomacy: Taxonomies and Histories. *The ANNALS of the American Academy of Political and Social Science, 616*(1), 31–54.

Dearnley, C. (2005). A Reflection on the Use of Semi-structured Interviews. *Nurse Researcher, 13*(1), 19–28.

Deitch, I. (2015, March 13). #AskHamas Twitter Campaign Backfires on Gaza Group. *The Times of Israel.*

Digital Disruption Short Fuse, Big Bang?. (2012). Australia: Deloitte Australia. Available online at http://www2.deloitte.com/content/dam/Deloitte/au/Documents/Building%20Lucky%20Country/deloitte-au-consulting-digital-disruption-whitepaper-0912.pdf.

Entman, R. M. (1993). Framing: Towards Clarification of a Fractured Paradigm. *McQuail's Reader in Mass Communication Theory*, 390–97.

———. (2003). Cascading Activation: Contesting the White House's Frame After 9/11. *Political Communication, 20*(4), 415–32.

———. (2008). Theorizing Mediated Public Diplomacy: The US Case. *The International Journal of Press/Politics, 13*(2), 87–102.

Eshet-Alkalai, Y. (2004). Digital Literacy: A Conceptual Framework for Survival Skills in the Digital Era. *Journal of Educational Multimedia and Hypermedia, 13*(1), 93–107.

Fan, Y. (2010). 'Branding the Nation: Towards a Better Understanding,' *Place Branding and Public Diplomacy,* 6(2), pp. 97–103.

Fisher, A. (2009). Four Seasons in One Day: The Crowded House of Public Diplomacy in the UK. *Routledge Handbook of Public Diplomacy, New York, Routledge*, 251–61.

———. (2010). Mapping the Great Beyond: Identifying Meaningful Networks in Public Diplomacy. *CPD Perspectives on Public Diplomacy,* 2, 1–87.

Fitzpatrick, K. R. (2007). Advancing the New Public Diplomacy: A Public Relations Perspective. *The Hague Journal of Diplomacy, 2*(3), 187–211.

Fontana, A., & Frey, J. (1994). The Art of Science. *The Handbook of Qualitative Research,* 361–76.

Golberg, A., & Kaduck, M. (2011). Where is Headquarters?: Diplomacy, Development and Defense. In J. G. Stein (Ed.), *Diplomacy in the Digital Age: Essays in Honour of Ambassador Allan Gotlieb* (pp. 125–40). Ontario: Signal.

Gravé-Lazi, L. (2014, July 16). IDC Fights War on Another Front. *The Jerusalem Post.* Retrieved from http://www.jpost.com/PromoContent/IDC-fights-war-on-another-front-362989.

Gregory, B. (2011). American Public Diplomacy: Enduring Characteristics, Elusive Transformation. *The Hague Journal of Diplomacy,* 6(3–4), 351–72.

Grunig, J. E., & Hunt, T. (1984). *Managing Public Relations* (Vol. 343). New York: Holt, Rinehart and Winston.

Hallams, E. (2010). Digital Diplomacy: The Internet, the Battle for Ideas & US Foreign Policy. *CEU Political Science Journal,* (04), 538–74.

Hamdy, N., & Gomaa, E. H. (2012). Framing the Egyptian Uprising in Arabic Language Newspapers and Social Media. *Journal of Communication,* 62(2), 195–211.

Harris, B. (2013). Diplomacy 2.0: The Future of Social Media in Nation Branding. *Exchange: The Journal of Public Diplomacy, 4*(1), 3.

Hayden, C. (2012). Social Media at State: Power, Practice, and Conceptual Limits for US Public Diplomacy. *Global Media Journal-American Edition, 11*(21).

Haynal, G. (2011). Corporate Diplomacy in the Information Age: Catching Up to the Dispersal of Power. In J. G. Stein (Ed.), *Diplomacy in the Digital Age: Essays in Honour of Ambassador Allan Gotlieb* (pp. 209–224). Ontario: Signal.

Hocking, B., & Melissen, J. (2015). *Diplomacy in the Digital Age, Cligendael Report.* Cligendeal Netherlands Institute of International Relations.

Hoffman, B. (2006, May 4). The Use of the Internet by Islamic Extremists. Testimony Presented to the House Permanent Select Committee on Intelligence, on May 4, 2006. Available online at http://www.rand.org/content/dam/rand/pubs/testimonies/2006/RAND_CT262-1.pdf.

Kampf, R., Manor, I., & Segev, E. (2015). Digital Diplomacy 2.0? A Cross-national Comparison of Public Engagement in Facebook and Twitter. *The Hague Journal of Diplomacy, 10*(4), 331–62.

Khatib, L., Dutton, W., & Thelwall, M. (2012). Public Diplomacy 2.0: A Case Study of the US Digital Outreach Team. *The Middle East Journal, 66*(3), 453–72.

Kent, M. L., & Taylor, M. (1998). Building Dialogic Relationships Through the World Wide Web. *Public Relations Rreview, 24*(3), 321–34.

Kotler, P. & Gertner, D. (2002). 'Country as Brand, Product, and Beyond: A Place Marketing and Brand Management Perspective,' *Brand Management, 9*(4–5), pp. 249–61.

Lee, G., & Kwak, Y. H. (2012). An Open Government Maturity Model for Social Media-based Public Engagement. *Government Information Quarterly, 29*(4), 492–503.

Leight, N., Walton, S. B., Ananian, T., Cruz-Enriquez, M., & Jarwaharlal, K. (2011). PDiN Quarterly—Trends in Public Diplomacy: January, February and March 2011. *Place Branding and Public Diplomacy, 7*(2), 136–49.

Lichtenstein, J. (2010, July 17). Digital Diplomacy. Retrieved July 4, 2015 from http://www.nytimes.com/2010/07/18/magazine/18web2-0-t.html.

Manor, I. (2015, January 4). How Kenya's MFA Leads by Example. *Exploring Digital Diplomacy* . Retrieved from http://digdipblog.com/2015/01/04/kenya/.

———. (2015, January 19). In Digital Diplomacy, a Narrowing Digital Divide—Part 1. *Exploring Digital Diplomacy*. Retrieved from http://digdipblog.com/2015/01/19/divide/.

———. (2015, March 15). On Hamas, Digital Diplomacy & Digital Hypocrisy. *Exploring Digital Diplomacy*. Retrieved from http://digdipblog.com/2015/03/15/on-hamas-digital-diplomacy-digital-hypocrisy/.

———. (2015, May 21). Digital Diplomacy During #NepalEarthquake. *Exploring Digital Diplomacy*. Retrieved from http://digdipblog.com/2015/05/21/digital-diplomacy-during-nepalearthquake/.

———. (2015, July 14). The Framing of #IranDeal on Digital Diplomacy Channels. *Exploring Digital Diplomacy*. Retrieved from http://digdipblog.com/2015/07/14/the-framing-of-irandeal-on-digital-diplomacy-channels/.

———. (2015, July 21). Is Digital Diplomacy Really Cost Effective? *Exploring Digital Diplomacy*. Retrieved from http://digdipblog.com/2015/07/21/is-digital-diplomacy-really-cost-effective/.

Manor, I., & Segev, E. (2015). America's Selfie: How the US Portrays Itself on its Social Media Accounts. In C. Bjola and M. Holmes (Eds.), *Digital Diplomacy Theory and Practice* (pp. 89–108). Oxon: Routledge.

Macnamara, J., Sakinofsky, P., & Beattie, J. (2012). E-electoral Engagement: How Governments Use Social Media to Engage Voters. *Australian Journal of Political Science, 47*(4), 623–39.

Macnamara, J. (2011). Pre and Post-election 2010 Online: What Happened to the Conversation?

Malone, D. (2011). New Friends in the Digital Age. In J. G. Stein (Ed.), *Diplomacy in the Digital Age* (pp. 102–24). Canada: McClelland & Stewart.

McNutt, K. (2014). Public Engagement in the Web 2.0 Era: Social Collaborative Technologies in a Public Sector Context. *Canadian Public Administration, 57*(1), 49–70.

Melissen, J. (2005). The New Public Diplomacy: Between Theory and Practice. In J. Melissen (Ed.), *The New Public Diplomacy: Soft Power in International Relations* (pp. 3–27). New York: Palgrave Macmillan.

Meraz, S., & Papacharissi, Z. (2013). Networked Gatekeeping and Networked Framing on #Egypt. *The International Journal of Press/Politics, 18*, 138–66.

Metzgar, E. T. (2012). Is it the Medium or the Message? Social Media, American Public Relations & Iran. *Global Media Journal*, 1–16.

Molad, the Center for Renewed Democracy. (2012). *Israeli Hasbara: Myths and Reality.* Jerusalem: Molad.

Natarajan, K. (2014). Digital Public Diplomacy and a Strategic Narrative for India. *Strategic Analysis, 38*(1), 91–106.

Ociepka, B. (2012). Impact of New Technologies on International Communication: The Case of Public Diplomacy. *Information Science*, (59), 24–36.

Ogawa. T. (2013). New Frontiers in Relational Public Diplomacy. In R. S. Zaharna, A. Arsenault & A. Fisher (Eds.), *Relational, Networked and Collaborative Approaches to Public Diplomacy: The Connective Mindshift* (pp. 117–31). Oxon: Rutledge.

Pamment, J. (2013). *New Public Diplomacy in the 21st Century*. New York: Rutledge.

———. (2015). Digital Diplomacy as Transmedia Engagement: Aligning Theories of Participatory Culture with International Advocacy Campaigns. *New Media & Society, 23* (1)1–17.

Papadopoulos, N., & Heslop, L. (2002). 'Country Equity and Country Branding: Problems and Prospects,' *Brand Management, 9*(4–5), pp. 294–314.

Park, H., & Reber, B. H. (2008). Relationship Building and the Use of Web Sites: How Fortune 500 Corporations Use Their Web Sites to Build Relationships. *Public Relations Review, 34*(4), 409–11.

Park, S. J., & Lim, Y. S. (2014). Information Networks and Social Media Use in Public Diplomacy: A Comparative Analysis of South Korea and Japan. *Asian Journal of Communication, 24*(1), 79–98.

Pew Research Center: The Evolving Role of News on Twitter and Facebook. (2015, July 14). Retrieved September 3, 2015 from http://www.journalism.org/2015/07/14/the-evolving-role-of-news-on-twitter-and-facebook/.

Porath, Z. (n.d.). *Letters from Jerusalem, 1947–1948*. Retrieved August 19, 2014, from http://www.zionism-israel.com/ezine/Partition_A_Night_To_Remember.htm.

Potter, E. H. (2002). *Managing Foreign Policy in the Twenty-First Century*. London: McGill-Queen's University Press.

Prensky, M. (2001). Digital natives, Digital Immigrants Part 1. *On the Horizon, 9*(5), 1–6.

Quelch, J. A., & Jocz, K. E. (2009). Can Brand Obama Rescue Brand America? *Brown J. World Aff., 16*, 163.

Quigley, K. (2013). 'Man Plans, God Laughs': Canada's National Strategy for Protecting Critical Infrastructure." *Canadian Public Administration 56*(1): 142–64.

Rana, K. S. (2013). Diaspora Diplomacy and Public Diplomacy. In R. S. Zaharna, A. Arsenault & A. Fisher (Eds.), *Relational, Networked and Collaborative Approaches to Public Diplomacy: The Connective Mindshift* (pp. 70–85). Oxon: Rutledge.

Ravid, B. Israel Opens Virtual Embassy to Gulf States. Retrieved August 21, 2014 from http://blogs.haaretz.co.il/barakravid/773/.

Saunders, H. H. (2013). The Relational Paradigm and Sustained Dialogue. In R. S. Zaharna, A. Arsenault & A. Fisher (Eds.), *Relational, Networked and Collaborative Approaches to Public Diplomacy: The Connective Mindshift* (pp. 132–43). Oxon: Routledge.

Scott, B. (n.d.). In Defense of #BringBackOurGirls and Hashtag Activism. Retrieved October 3, 2015, from http://www.slate.com/blogs/future_tense/2014/05/16/bringbackourgirls_a_defense_of_hashtag_activism.html.

Scott, J. (2012). 'Bill 3 & Privacy Implications.' *Canadian Journal of Administrative Law & Practice 25* (3): 209–35.

Seib, P. (2012). *Real-time Diplomacy: Politics and Power in the Social Media Era*. Palgrave Macmillan.

Seo, H. (2013). The 'Virtual Last Three Feet.' In R. S. Zaharna, A. Arsenault & A. Fisher (Eds.), *Relational, Networked and Collaborative Approaches to Public Diplomacy: The Connective Mindshift* (pp. 157–69). Oxon: Routledge.

Sharp, P. (2005). Revolutionary States, Outlaw Regimes and the Techniques of Public Diplomacy. In J. Melissen (Ed.), *The New Public Diplomacy: Soft Power in International Relations* (pp. 106–24). New York: Palgrave Macmillan.

Shenhav, S. R., Sheafer, T., & Gabay, I. (2010). Incoherent narrator: Israeli public diplomacy during the disengagement and the elections in the Palestinian Authority. *israel studies, 15*(3), 143–62.

Slaughter, A. M. (2009). America's Edge. *Foreign Affairs, 88*(1), 94–113.

Smith, B. G. (2010). Socially Distributing Public Relations: Twitter, Haiti, and Interactivity in Social Media. *Public Relations Review, 36*(4), 329–35.

Stoltzfus, K. (2008). Exploring US E-diplomacy and Non-state Actors' Increasing Communicative Influence. In *Proceedings of the 2008 International Conference on Digital Government Research* (pp. 347–54).

Sotiriu, S. (2015). Digital Diplomacy: Between Promises and Reality. In C. Bjola, M. Holmes (Ed.), *Digital Diplomacy* (pp. 33–51). New York: Routledge.

Stein, J. G. (2011). Introduction. In J. G. Stein (Ed.), *Diplomacy in the Digital Age* (pp. 1–9). Canada: McClelland & Stewart.

Stockton, N. (2015, August 23). NASA's Social Media Strategy Is Genius—And Kinda Maddening. Retrieved August 26, 2015, from http://www.wired.com/2015/07/nasas-social-media-strategy-genius-kinda-maddening/.

Toosi, N. (2015). White House to Engage Iran Critics Through @TheIranDeal. Retrieved September 12, 2015, from http://www.politico.com/story/2015/07/white-house-to-engage-iran-critics-through-theirandeal-120408.html.

The Economist. (2012, September 22). Virtual Realtions. *The Economist.* Retrieved from http://www.economist.com/node/21563284.

———. (2007, July 21). God's Ambassadors. *The Economist.* Retrieved September 5, 2015, from http://www.economist.com/node/9516461.

The White House. (2009). *Remarks by President Obama on a New Beginning.* Retrieved July 13, 2014, from http://www.whitehouse.gov/the_press_office/Remarks-by-the-President-at-Cairo-University-6-04-09.

Twiploamcy. (2015). *Twiplomacy Study 2015.* Retrieved July 13, 2015.

United States Advisory Commission on Public Diplomacy (2015). 2015 Comprehensive Annual Report on Public Diplomacy and International Broadcasting. Retrieved August 13, 2015, from http://www.state.gov/documents/organization/247329.pdf.

US Army. (2014). *FM-3-24 and MCWP 3-33.5 Insurgencies and Countering Insurgencies.* Washington, D.C.: Headquarters, Department of the Army. Available online at https://fas.org/irp/doddir/army/fm3-24.pdf.

Van Ham, P. (2013). Social Power in Public Diplomacy. In R. S. Zaharna, A. Arsenault & A. Fisher (Eds.), *Relational, Networked and Collaborative Approaches to Public Diplomacy: The Connective Mindshift* (pp. 17–28). Oxon: Routledge.

Vanc, A. M. (2012). Post-9/11 US Public Diplomacy in Eastern Europe: Dialogue via New Technologies or Face-to-Face Communication? *Global Media Journal—American Edition, 11* (21).

Waters, R. D., Burnett, E., Lamm, A., & Lucas, J. (2009). Engaging Stakeholders Through Social Networking: How Nonprofit Organizations Are Using Facebook. *Public Relations Review, 35*(2), 102–06.

Wehrenfennig, D. (2012). From an Analog Past to a Digital Future: Information and Communication Technology in Conflict Managment. In *Cyberspace and Global Affairs* (pp. 23–50). Surrey: Ashgate Publishing Limited.

Wendt, A. (1998). On Constitution and Causation in International Relations. *Review of International Studies, 24*(05), 101–18.

Whiting, L. S. (2008). Semi-structured Interviews: Guidance for Novice Researchers. *Nursing Standard, 22*(23), 35.

Williamson, W. F., & Kelley, J. R. (2012). #Kelleypd: Public Diplomacy 2.0 Classroom. *Global Media Journal—American Edition, 11*(21).

Wichowski, A. (2015). 'Secrecy is for Losers': Why Diplomats Should Embrace Openness to Protect National Security. In C. Bjola and M. Holmes (Eds.), *Digital Diplomacy Theory and Practice* (pp. 52–70). Oxon: Routledge.

Xiguang, L., & Jing, W. (2010). Web-based Public Diplomacy: The Role of Social Media in the Iranian and Xinjiang Riots. *Journal of International Communication, 16*(1), 7–22.

Zaharna, R. S., & Rugh, W. A. (2012). Issue Theme: The Use of Social Media in U.S. Public Diplomacy. *Global Media Journal—American Edition, 11*(21), 1–8.

Zaharna, R. S., Arsenault, E., & Fisher, A. (2013). The Connective Mindshift. In R. S. Zaharna, A. Arsenault & A. Fisher (Eds.), *Relational, Networked and Collaborative Approaches to Public Diplomacy: The Connective Mindshift* (pp. 144–56). Oxon: Routledge.

Zaharna, R. S. (2013). Network Purpose, Network Design: Dimensions of Network and Collaborative Public Diplomacy. In R. S. Zaharna, A. Arsenault & A. Fisher (Eds.), *Relational, Networked and Collaborative Approaches to Public Diplomacy: The Connective Mindshift* (pp. 173–89). Oxon: Routledge.

Zhang, J. (2013). A Strategic Issue Management (SIM) Approach to Social Media Use in Public Diplomacy. *American Behavioral Scientist, 57*(9), 1312–31.

Appendix 1: Entman's Cascading Activation Model (2003)

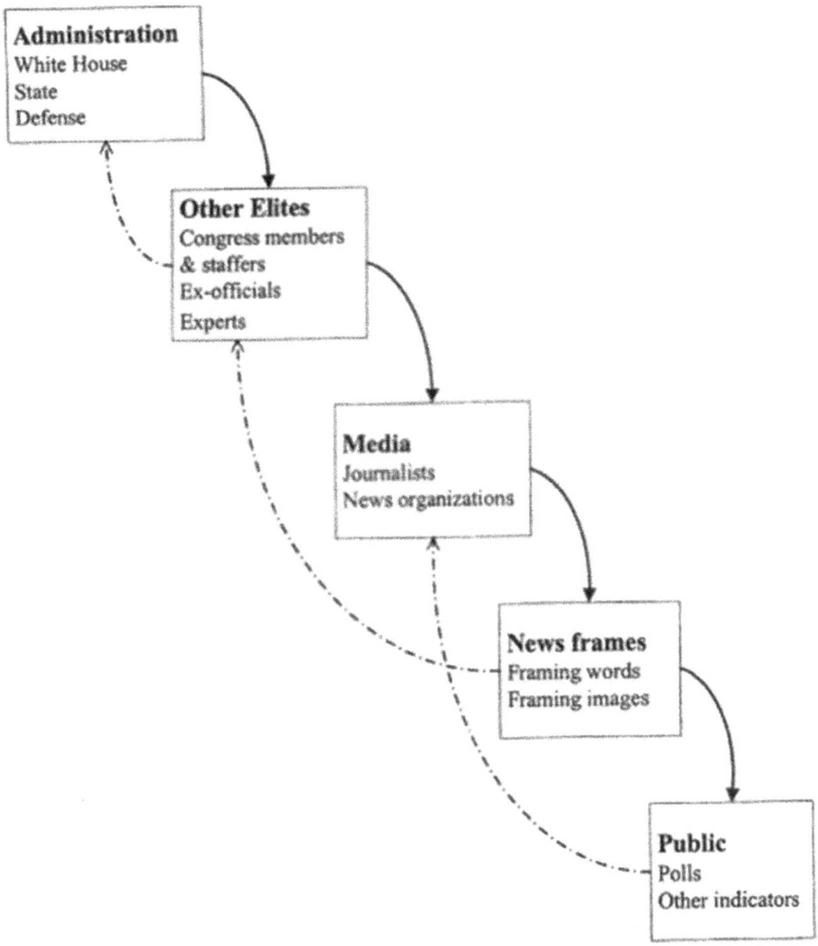

Appendix 2: Guide Used in Interview with Head of Digital Diplomacy Unit—Israeli Ministry of Foreign Affairs

1. How is the digital diplomacy unit structured? To what department does it belong?
2. Are there departments within the unit? What are the areas of responsibility of each sub-department?
3. Who heads the digital diplomacy unit? Trained diplomat? Social Media expert?

4. How does the digital diplomacy unit communicate with other departments in the MFA (scheduled meetings, debriefings, inter-office mails)?
5. Who actually formulates tweets and Facebook posts?
6. How does the digital diplomacy unit work with social media managers at the embassy level? Do they oversee all activity or do they visit embassy twitter profiles every few days or so?
7. How do you define engagement in digital diplomacy?
8. Is engagement with followers important to your MFA? Are you encouraged to engage with followers? Or is it forbidden?
9. Who in the digital diplomacy unit is in charge of engagement with followers?
10. How does the ministry deal with the fact that other national organizations are also active on social media (e.g., prime minister, ministry of defense, president)? Is there coordination of messages between all these parties?
11. Does the ministry operate more than one Twitter channel or Facebook page? If so, why?
12. Has the medium changed the message? Does digital diplomacy bring with it a new sort of message?
13. Do you know who follows your social media accounts? Do you know who your audience is de-facto?
14. Do you use Twitter accounts of other embassies or diplomats to gather relevant information?
15. Can you give me an example of how you can use the advantages of digital tools to reach target audiences?

Appendix 3: Final Interview Guide

1. How do you define digital diplomacy?
2. How is the digital diplomacy unit structured? To what department does it belong?
3. Are there departments within the unit? What are the areas of responsibility of each sub-department?
4. Who heads the digital diplomacy unit? Trained diplomat? Social media expert? Why?
5. Do you work with external social media agencies or experts?
6. How does the digital diplomacy unit communicate with other departments in the MFA (scheduled meetings, debriefings, inter-office mails)?
7. Who actually formulates tweets and Facebook posts?
8. Who decides what issues will be featured on digital diplomacy at the ministry level?

9. Who decides what issues will be featured on digital diplomacy at the embassy level?
10. How does the digital diplomacy unit work with social media managers at the embassy level? Do they oversee all activity or do they visit embassy Twitter profiles every few days or so?
11. Do embassies include SNS content when reporting back to the ministry?
12. How do you define engagement in digital diplomacy?
13. Is engagement with followers important to your MFA? Are you encouraged to engage with followers? Or is it forbidden?
14. Who in the digital diplomacy unit is in charge of engagement with followers?
15. How do you measure digital diplomacy activity? What parameters are used? What metrics?
16. How often do you evaluate digital diplomacy efficacy? Do embassies do this as well?
17. How do you measure engagement with followers? Do you measure it?
18. Do you define target audiences when practicing digital diplomacy (global audience, reporters, other MFAs)?
19. Can you give me an example of how you can use the advantages of digital tools to reach target audiences?
20. Do you know who follows your social media accounts? Do you know who your audience is de-facto?
21. How does the ministry deal with the fact that other national organizations are also active on social media (e.g., prime minister, ministry of defense, president)? Is there coordination of messages between all these parties?
22. Does the ministry operate more than one Twitter channel or Facebook page? If so, why?
23. Do you use Twitter accounts of other embassies or diplomats to gather relevant information?
24. Has the medium changed the message? Does digital diplomacy bring with it a new sort of message?

Appendix 4: Questionnaire for MFA Level Digital Diplomacy Staffer

Exploring Digital Diplomacy—MFA Level

Below is a questionnaire that deals with digital diplomacy activity at your MFA/embassy. We kindly ask that you take a few moments to answer the questions below. Many thanks, Ilan.

1. How is the digital diplomacy unit structured? To what department does it belong?
2. How many people comprise the digital diplomacy unit?
3. Are there departments within the unit? What are the areas of responsibility of each sub-department?
4. What other departments does the digital diplomacy unit work with (e.g., spokesperson, media affairs)?
5. Who heads the digital diplomacy unit? Trained diplomat? Social media expert?
6. Who work at the digital diplomacy unit? Is it made up of trained diplomats or social media experts?
7. How does the digital diplomacy unit communicate with other departments in the MFA (scheduled meetings, debriefings, inter-office mails)?
8. Who actually formulates tweets and Facebook posts? What age are they?
9. Do people who formulate tweets have autonomy? Or is there a procedure to be followed before each tweet or post is written and posted?
10. Who decides what topics will be addressed in tweets and posts? Members of the digital diplomacy teams? Other departments? Head of digital diplomacy unit?
11. Do the same people write all tweets and posts? Or does each department write its own tweet (e.g., Africa desk, Europe Desk)?
12. Who decides what hashtags (#) will be used or promoted?
13. How does the digital diplomacy unit work with social media managers at the embassy level? Do they oversee all activity or do they visit embassy Twitter profiles every few days or so?
14. Does the ministry authorize every tweet or post published at the embassy level?
15. How often does the digital diplomacy unit at the ministry communicate with social media managers at the embassy level?
16. Are there tweets or posts that are global (i.e., tweeted by the ministry and all its embassies around the world at the same time)? If so, what sort of messages?
17. What topics are considered to be important on a "global" scale?
18 How do you define engagement in digital diplomacy?
19. Is engagement with followers important to your MFA? Are you encouraged to engage with followers? Or is it forbidden?
20. Who in the digital diplomacy unit is in charge of engagement with followers?
21. Does the ministry place an emphasis on engaging with followers who criticize your country? If so, why?
22. Is there a feedback mechanism in which comments on tweets or posts are taken into account when formulating new tweets?
23. Does the ministry regularly analyze its followers? If so, what parameters are important (e.g., total number of followers, type of followers such as journalists from major newspapers or other foreign ministries)?

24. Are comments posted online sent to relevant departments (e.g., criticism posted online with regard to policy in a specific area or country sent to department in charge of that country at MFA)?
25. Are the same messages tweeted and posted on Facebook and other platforms? If so, why? Why not make different use of each medium?
26. On what SNS is your MFA active (e.g., Twitter, Facebook, Instagram)?
27. How does the ministry deal with the fact that other national organizations are also active on social media (e.g., prime minister, ministry of defense, president)? Is there coordination of messages between all these parties?
28. Does the ministry operate more than one Twitter channel or Facebook page? If so, why?

Appendix 5: Questionnaire for Embassy Digital Diplomacy Manager

Exploring Digital Diplomacy—Embassy Level

Below is a questionnaire that deals with digital diplomacy activity at your MFA/embassy. We kindly ask that you take a few moments to answer the questions below. Many thanks, Ilan.

1. Are you a trained diplomat or a local employee working at an embassy abroad? What age are you?
2. To whom do you report within the embassy? Who is your supervisor? To what department in the embassy do you belong?
3. How do you decide what topics to address in tweets or Facebook posts? Is it your decision? Your supervisor's? The ministry's?
4. Do you have autonomy with regard to which tweets or posts to publish? Or do you need authorization from the ministry for each post and tweet?
5. Do you receive information from other employees in the embassy which is used in tweets and posts? If so, how often do you receive such information?
6. How do you communicate with other departments in the embassy (scheduled meetings, emails, special de-briefings)?
7. What percentage of the posts and tweets published by the embassy are formulated by the ministry? What percentage is formulated by you?
8. Do you re-phrase tweets and posts formulated by the ministry or do you simply re-tweet them? Why do you re-phrase them?
9. Which language do you use? Local one? English?
10. How do you define engagement in digital diplomacy?
11. What emphasis is placed on engagement at your ministry?

12. How often do you find yourself engaging with followers (e.g., answering questions, supplying information)?
13. Is there are priority to engaging with those who criticize your country? Or is it forbidden?
14. Do comments you receive on tweets or posts you publish impact future digital tweets and posts? If so, in what way?
15. Do other diplomats at the embassy tweet? Do they do so on the embassy's account or their own?
16. How often do you communicate with the digital diplomacy unit at ministry level? To what purpose to you communicate with the unit?
17. How you know what topics are regarded as a priority by the ministry?
18. How often do you analyze your audience base?
19. What audience are you trying to attract to the embassy digital diplomacy channels (local press, local population)?
20. In the past, the embassy spokesperson was in charge of disseminating messages to the press. What role does he play in the age of digital diplomacy when reporters follow social media accounts?
21. Which areas are more relevant in each social network (Twitter/Facebook)? Political diplomacy? Investment promotions? Cultural issues? Consular affairs?

www.ingramcontent.com/pod-product-compliance
Lightning Source LLC
Chambersburg PA
CBHW071353230926
51846CB00002B/531